Ask. Believe. Receive.

Our Power to Create Our Own Destiny

Raymond E. Lumsden

Freebird Publishers

North Dighton, MA

i

Freebird Publishers

221 Pearl St., Ste. 541, North Dighton, MA 02764
Info@FreebirdPublishers.com
www.FreebirdPublishers.com

Copyright © 2020
Ask. Believe. Receive.
By Raymond E. Lumsden

All Freebird Publishers titles, imprints, and distributed lines are available at special quantity discounts for bulk purchases for sales promotions, premiums, fundraising, and educational or institutional use.

ISBN: 978-1-952159-09-1

Printed in the United States of America

In memory of my grandmother, Isabelle Lumsden,

and my grandfather, Raymond R. Lumsden.

I miss you both.

A man's future consists of the faith inside of him. Whatever that faith is, so shall it become his reality.

– The Bhagavagita

Foreword

First and foremost, this is a book about survival and hope.

A man named Nietzche once said, "He who has a way to live for can bear almost any How." Where there is hope, there will always be a future for its holder.

The philosopher Freud believed that life isn't primarily a quest for pleasure or a quest for power, but instead...a quest for meaning. As people, we require a direction and a purpose for our existence, or we are likely to fall into despair. But life doesn't always give us straight and narrow roads to navigate, and we often find ourselves lost along the way.

Forces beyond our control can sometimes take away everything we own, with the exception of our freedom to choose how we will respond to any given situation and hardship we encounter in our lives. We cannot always choose what will happen to us in life, but we can always control what we feel and how we respond to what happens to us in our lives.

This book is meant to offer hope to its readers, to encourage those who are lost or battling life's trials and tribulations, and to encourage you to find your purpose and the strength to achieve that purpose.

I have chosen to use my own experiences as an example, even where I have failed miserably in my life, to show that there aren't any exceptions to the rules. There aren't any perfect people, and we are all sinners in our own right.

But the one thing we all share embedded deep in our souls is the spirit of hope and the ability to overcome.

My grandfather used to tell me as a child, "If you believe it, you can then achieve it." He would make me verbally say the things I wanted to overcome or accomplish so as to give "birth" to it and to make it a reality.

To this day, I still do so, and I hope that you will learn how to tap into your own strength and, in doing so, achieve your intended purpose in life. That you will remember your human dignity, love, peace, and hope in all things.

Through our positive words, we can activate our creative power and bring forth those things into existence. Through the Laws of Attraction, we can control our destinies and fate. Genesis tells us that we are created in the image of God, therefore, God's ourselves. I challenge you to then tap into your Godly power and take control of your lives for the better.

If only I knew years ago what I have come to know today. In these pages, I will now share that newly found wisdom with you.

Let me now prove to you that you are indeed...a god, that you can create your own destiny and life through your words.

Ask, Believe, Receive – it's as simple as that.

Table of Contents

Life IS NOT ABOUT WAITING FOR THE STORM TO PASS BUT LEARNING TO DANCE IN THE RAIN

Chapter 1: The Basics

The word Bible stems from the Greek word meaning "Books." In truth, the Bible is actually two collections of books, known to most as the "New Testament" and the "Old Testament." The word "testament" was used to mean a covenant or agreement. It refers to God's promise to us, his people.

The Old Testament is the collection of writings that relate to the agreement that God made with the descendants of Jacob, in the time of Moses. The New Testament is the collection of writings relating to God's agreements with all people who believe in Jesus Christ.

The Old Testament talks about the great things God did for the people of Israel and his plan for them as his chosen people to bring his blessings to the whole world. These writings promise the coming of a savior, or "Messiah." The Old Testament is important for understanding the New Testament because it provides the necessary background. And the New Testament completes the story of salvation that began in the Old Testament.

The writings in the Old Testament are made up of a collection of thirty-nine different books produced by many different authors. Originally, they were written in Hebrew, the language of ancient Israel. There are a few sections in Aramaic and international language in Bible times. Years passed in between the writing of the first book and the last. The Old Testament has books of law, history, prose, songs, poetry, and wisdom quotes.

The Old Testament is usually divided into three main sections: the Law, the Prophets, and the Holy Writings. The Law contains the five books called "The Five Books of Moses." The first book

is Genesis. It tells about the beginning of the world as we know it, the first man and woman, and their first sin against God that changed everything. It tells about the Great Flood and the family God saved through that flood, and it talks about the beginning of the nation of Israel, the people God chose to use for a special purpose.

Today's readers of the Bible, a lot like me, need to keep in mind that these books were written thousands of years ago for people who lived in cultures very different from what we live in today. Because of the gap in time between their world and our own, you will likely find parts of the Bible hard to believe and at the very least, very strange.

To acquire a better understanding of the ancient customs, some research into information about life in those times would be very helpful. The lessons to be learned from biblical accounts are important at any age. For example, Jesus told a story about a man sowing grain in a field that had different types of soil conditions. Those exact conditions may be unfamiliar to farmers today, but the lesson drawn from the story is meaningful everywhere today because it deals with people's basic spiritual needs, which never change.

If you read the Bible with an open mind, which I still struggle with, you can expect to receive many benefits. You will gain knowledge about the history and culture of the ancient world, you will learn about Jesus and his teachings for mankind, and what following Jesus will bring to you. You will learn practical lessons for living a dynamic and joy-filled life and may find answers to life's most difficult questions. There are, therefore, many good reasons for reading the Bible, and if you read it with a sincere and receptive spirit and heart, you just may discover God's purpose for your life.

The commitment to follow Jesus is the most important decision you will ever make if that is where reading the Bible takes you. It is not a simple decision like deciding what to eat or what to wear. It is even more important than choosing what political party you should associate with or whom you may want to marry. If reading the Bible brings you to spirituality and the decision to give your heart to Jesus, that is a life and death decision, both in this life and in the next, according to the scripture.

Admittedly, that is a decision I continue to struggle with daily due to my strong understanding and "belief" in the sciences, where we are able to prove so much. But, then again, perhaps science is one of the abilities given to us by God, the same as everything else we are capable of doing. You see...my struggle is real.

Which leads to my next point: what if reading the Bible expands your mind and understanding of life? Is that a bad thing even if you aren't swayed to drop on your knees and confess your devotion to Jesus Christ? In truth, that's my whole purpose for writing this book: to express my views, thoughts, and interpretations after having read the Bible cover-to-cover more than twenty times over the past five years.

I mean, let's imagine for the next year that you do nothing to improve yourself and don't read the Bible. A year from today, you will have the same understanding and education that you have today, but you will be a year older. And so, what have you got to lose? Also, how are you to make the determination as to whether you agree with my views expressed in this book unless you read the Bible and see for yourself?

Now, today is the time to take positive steps to grow your mind so that you may be better prepared for life. Invest the time you would usually waste watching television or other unimportant things and put forth the effort to improve yourself. And just perhaps...save your soul in the process, should you come to believe.

And just maybe...you will be able to eliminate stress, hardship, and the daily ups and downs we all experience and find peace.

If you have children or are planning to have children, wouldn't you want to ensure that they have a clean slate? That there may exist a means to protect them from your past "demons" and transgressions? Well, from my understanding of the biblical texts, such a means is available to us within Jesus Christ. And so, even if we end up being wrong, and religion is what some believe it to be, a bunch of hocus pocus system of control, what is there to lose?

Additionally, what if you possess a far greater "power" than you could ever imagine, or would ever have believed to be true? What if the answers to your most complicated issues and hardships exist within you already – the power to heal, create life, change the outcome of situations, change the future, accomplish the impossible, etc.?

Well...you do. The reason for that is quite simple: if you read the Bible and believe its scriptures,

We are all God's, according to God himself.

Allow me to prove that...if, of course, you believe.

Notes:

Chapter 2: **Words of Power**

Words are the containers that carry the substance of our faith. If you speak words of faith, you activate the positive side of that force; if you speak words of fear and apprehension, you activate the negative side of the force. This is called making confessions.

Everything that happens to us is a direct result of our words. In the beginning, God created the universe, earth, and man...with only his words, if you believe the scripture. He simply spoke everything into existence with the force of faith, as I have come to understand it.

Hebrews 11:1 says, "Now faith is the substance of things hoped for, the evidence of things not seen." Therefore, I take that to mean that faith...is a substance of literal means. It's the "basic stuff" out of which the entire universe is made and the raw material substance that the spirit of God used to form the universe.

Therefore, everything we touch is made out of molecules, which in turn are made out of atoms, which are composed of subatomic particles, which comprise this thing called faith. Virtually everything would then be made up of faith.

In Luke 1:5-80, God was so certain of the power of words that he even rendered Zechariah speechless so as to not interfere with his plan. There, Zechariah questioned God, saying, "Are you really sure this is going to happen, Lord? How can I be sure of this since we are so old? I just don't believe it is possible." In response, Gabriel, having been sent by God as his messenger to Zechariah, said, "You will be silent and not able to speak until the day this happens because you do not believe my words, which will come true in faith."

There would be no purpose in taking away Zechariah's speech but for the possibility that his words could interfere with and, perhaps, defeat the will of God. I know, right now, you are probably rolling your eyes and thinking, "How can a human be more powerful than God?" But a quick look at Genesis 3:22 reveals, "Then the Lord God said, "The man has become like one of us; like me; he knows good and evil. We must keep him from eating some of the fruit from the tree of life, or he will live forever."

Hmmmm...so, how could a human live forever? And who was God talking to?

Perhaps a look at Max Lucado's book, *In the Eye of the Storm*, gives us the answers to those questions. In his book, Lucado points out:

"He placed one scoop of clay upon another until a form lay lifeless on the ground...all were silent as the Creator reached inside of himself and removed something yet unseen. It's called 'choice,' the seed of choice.

Creation stood still in silence and gazed upon the lifeless form.

An angel spoke, "But what if he ..."

"What if he chooses not to love?" The Creator finished. "Come, I will show you."

Unbound by today, God and the angel walked into tomorrow...The angel gasped at what he saw – spontaneous love, voluntary devotion – never had he seen anything like this.

The angel stood speechless as they passed through centuries of repugnance. Never had the angel seen such filth, rotten hearts, ruptured promises, and forgotten loyalties.

"Wouldn't it be better to not plant the seed? Wouldn't it be easier to not give the choice?"

"It would," the Creator spoke slowly. "But to remove the choice is to remove the love."

They stepped into the Garden again. The Maker looked earnestly at the clay creation. A monsoon of love swelled up within him. He had died for the creation before he had even made him. God's form bent over the sculpted face and breathed.

Dust stirred on the lips of the new one. The chest rose, cracking the red mud. The cheeks fleshened. A finger moved. And an eye opened. But more incredible than the moving of the flesh was the stirring of the spirit. Those who could see the unseen gasped.

"It looks like...it appears so much like...it is him!"

The angel wasn't speaking of the face, the features, or the body. He was looking inside - at the soul.

"It's eternal!" gasped another.

Within the man, God had placed a divine seed, a seed of Himself. The creator had created not a creature, but another creator."

And so, when God said in Genesis 3:22, "The man has become like one of us," he was speaking to another divine entity and meant that we were also divine. Gods and Creators, like himself.

And so, Gabriel, when speaking to Zechariah about God's plan for him and his wife, took away his "power" to speak so as to not thwart God's plan with the power inside of his words.

Our words are vital in bringing our dreams to reality. Speaking words of faith over our lives in a positive affirmation brings positive and long-term change. Whether it's health, wealth, business achievement, our children, or whatever it may be, we have the inherent power to speak it into existence. On the flip side, our words can also bring negative outcomes where we speak doubt, apprehension, and uncertainty,

The thoughts and feelings that you profess into the world, good or bad, are exactly what will be coming back to you. Ultimately, you will have the world that you created through your words, as well as your faith or lack thereof.

I may submit further that the law of attraction is the law of creation. Quantum physicists tell us that the entire universe emerged from thought, and that we create our lives through our thoughts and the law of attraction. While the science of quantum physics is well beyond my complete understanding and very complex, it is allegedly relatively simple to apply. In fact, the New Testament teaches us, "Ask, Believe, Receive."

In a nutshell, thoughts and verbal announcements are the primary cause of everything in our lives, whether good or bad. Whatever has happened or will happen to us is a direct cause of our faith expressed. Faith is a force; words are the containers of that force, and through that force, we can control and create our own destiny.

Going back to the story of Zechariah, God knew the power of our words and our ability to prophesy our future since he blew his power into us at creation. He knew that Zechariah's negative words would cancel out his plan – the proverbial "law of attraction" at work.

I do not personally believe that a simple thought...can achieve the same outcome as a spoken word. Our words are vital in bringing our wishes to fruition. It's not enough to simply see it in faith or in your imagination. We must actually speak the words into the world in order to bring forth action. Our spoken words have tremendous power, especially creatively. The moment we speak something out loud, we give "birth" to it. This, of course, is a spiritual principle.

Take, for instance, the Jewish people during the German occupation. While it may seem incomprehensible that multitudes of people could have been responsible for attracting the massacre, the fact remains that it's quite possible if you believe in scripture. If the Jewish multitudes were of the mindset of being in the wrong place at the wrong time, and that they had no control over outside circumstances, and that they verbally spoke those feelings into the world, then those words of fear, defeat, and powerlessness would create their destiny.

Nothing, according to scripture and faith, from what I've been able to decipher, can come into our existence/experience unless we summon it with our thoughts and words. Native American people believe this also, and have for thousands of years, which is why they chant when they pray. They believe that their thoughts are carried with the chanting, into the smoke of the sweat lodge, and up to their ancestors or the creator.

Consider again another biblical example of the power that spoken words have over our lives: the story of Abraham and Sarah. Like Zechariah and his wife Elizabeth, Abraham and Sarah were very old. The moment that God told Sarah that she would have a child, Sarah, who saw herself as an old lady and barren, began making negative comments and confessions. Because of the power of her spoken confessions to the negative faith, God had to take action. And so, he changed her name from Sarah to Sarai, which means 'princess.' After hearing her new name over time, she began to think of herself as a younger woman, which in turn changed her self-image. When her self-image was changed, she began to have positive confessions, which then triggered the law of attraction. As God intended, she gave birth.

As people, we use the law of attraction and spoken words every day, whether we know it or not. Our words go out of our mouths, and they come right back into our ears. When we hear those words enough, for long enough, they drop down into our spirit, and they produce what we say: when we are running that last mile on the treadmill, and we will ourselves to keep going while our bodies are screaming to stop; when we are trying to gather the courage to speak in front of a group of people or to ask a client for a sale, and we whisper out loud, "I can do this."

And as further evidence that verbal words and sounds are the key to obtaining our wishes, needs, and wants…and that we are born with the "power" to speak things into existence…look no further than a newborn baby. There's no other way to put it: a newborn baby might just be the most powerful of us all. The ability of the neonate to impose its will on others and to make things happen is second to none. Now, you may be saying to yourself, "But newborns don't talk." However, in their minds and purposes, they sure do. I'll explain further in just a moment.

The amazing thing is that the human response to infants is pretty much universal across any demographic. Culture, age, sex- you name it, the reaction is almost identical. Take age. Studies have shown that infants as young as four days old can form sounds that they use repetitively to obtain their quest if you will. That quest is to influence those around them to take care of them. Absent those sounds and "verbal" requests known as the cry, they could very well be forgotten and die. This is why the infant uses various tones, volumes, and durations to achieve different results. Those of us with children will easily understand the difference between a dirty diaper cry...and a hungry cry. In those respects, the infants are talking into the universe, using the law of attraction.

And so, since it's there from birth, the ability to achieve our desires and create our destiny through "words" and thoughts must be divine.

And did you know that when you are born again, you're not a citizen of this world? You may be living in it right now, operating in this world, but you are not of this world. When you are born again, your citizenship is in heaven... (Philippians 3: 20, New King James Version). You are then born of God, and spiritually, you've been translated into his kingdom. At this very moment, while you are walking around on this earth in your physical body, God's kingdom is living inside of you; you're living in it, and you have access to all its resources, rights, and privileges.

You don't need to worry about a single thing on this earth. If you'll simply walk in the power of your heavenly citizenship, you can overcome any challenge or hardship this world throws at you. You can rise above all difficult circumstances. You can triumph over all trouble the devil stirs up in this world. You can live as more than a conqueror and walk out your days here in victory instead of defeat. That is what the Bible tells us.

To do that, however, you can't just go around thinking and talking like the rest of the world does. You have to maintain a spirit of faith. You must keep your heart full of God's Word so that when bad news comes your way, and it will, rather than giving in to fear and panic or discouragement, you can say what God says about the situation.

He's already spoken about every need we could ever have and every known problem any of us will ever face. In the Bible, he has laid out the way for us to experience the "days of heaven upon the earth" (Deuteronomy 11:21). Every one of those words became law in the spirit realm the moment they were spoken, and even though they've been in the scriptures for thousands of years, they still have God's Spirit and life in them. Everything God ever said is still true, and any of us can believe it, say it, and act on it, and it will come to pass. Of course, you have to be a believer.

As a believer, however, you won't always want to do that. Particularly when we're in a hard place, we sometimes just want to give up, give into our flesh and talk about the problem. Rather than opening our Bibles and standing on God's Word, we want Him to do *for* us what He told us to do. I, for one, am extremely guilty of this, especially in my current situation and surroundings of extreme hardship. Add to that my confessed internal and mental struggle with my own faith and belief, and I'm pretty much a mess.

Sometimes, we want God to speak faith over our lives by sending someone to tell us that our problems have been or will be resolved that we are healed, or over the financial difficulty. We want God to command the mountains in our lives to move while we sit around having a pity party and spouting disbelief into the world, engaging the law of attraction to the negative force. But that's not how the Bible tells us it works. It's not set up to manifest on earth simply in response to God's words. It's designed instead to respond to *our* words, at least according to the New Testament.

According to scripture, the devil flees when we resist him, saying, like Jesus did, "It is written" (James 4:7; Matthew 4:4). The mountains in our lives only move when we have "faith" and speak it out loud. "For whosoever shall say unto this mountain, be thou removed, and be cast into the sea; and shall believe that those things which he sayeth shall come to pass; he shall have whatsoever he sayeth. (Mark 11:22-23). For God's will to manifest in our lives, we must speak his words out loud by faith, as it tells us in 2 Corinthians 4:13.

We bring heaven to earth not by complaining about the things down here that are giving us problems but by having a "spirit of faith, according as it is written, I believed, and therefore have I spoken; we also believe, and therefore speak" (2 Corinthians 4:13).

Does all of this mean that God will just do whatever we say? Not exactly. What it does mean, according to Scripture, is that God will do what we say by *faith*, which comes by hearing the Word of God. Confusing, right?

If God hasn't said a particular thing is His will, we don't have a basis for expecting Him to do it. On the contrary, if He said it, we could believe it, speak it, and expect to receive it. Why? Because it's His Word, and "the Word that God speaks is alive and full of power…active, operative, energizing, and effective" (Hebrews 4:12, Amplified Bible).

God's word contains His creative power. It contained that power when it first came out of His mouth, and if we get it inside of us and let it abide in our hearts, it will come out of our mouths with the same kind of creative power and faith it had when God first spoke it. Think of it like a cycle. God sends down His Word to us, and then we renew our minds with it and learn to think about things the way He does. As we learn to think like Him, we begin to talk like Him. We believe and speak His Words, and they produce His results. Does that make sense? It actually does to me as well, yet I still continue to struggle in applying it.

If you read the Bible, you can seek out what His will is in every aspect of life. You can find his promises and apply them to whatever situation may be in your life. Then, receive them as your own, get them into your heart in abundance, and keep saying them out loud in faith until they manifest. This is how God intends for all of us, as believers, of course, to live every day. He intends for us to make His Word our number one priority and spend time in it daily. Remember, Jesus said in John 15:7, "If ye abide in me, and my words abide in you, ye shall ask what ye will, and it shall be done unto you."

The Word that abides in us is the Word that talks to us, good or bad. It's the Word that comes up in us when the world throws us a curve ball and the devil comes knocking. That's how you know a drunk person usually means what they say while drunk, since there isn't a "filter" at that time, and the Word in his heart comes out. We...usually say what we are made of what's in our heart. We, as in people, are not drunks since I don't drink.

In Matthew 12:34, that very truth is detailed: "For out of the abundance of the heart the mouth speaketh." Our lives depend on what we have in our hearts. So, keep it filled with God's Word. Then, when trouble hits, and it will, you'll be ready. You'll be in the habit of talking like God does, and you won't be easy prey for the devil. He is always trying to get hold of our tongues, which he usually succeeds in my case, so we will make mistakes and profess negative faith in the world, therefore making it happen.

As a believer, if you do, in fact, believe, we don't want the devil to get to us like that. We don't want him tricking our tongues into disbelief and doubt. Especially where hope is all that a person has; such is the case in my particular situation, in prison, fighting for my innocence. What we say determines our course of life. It is written in James 3:4-5.

Our words are powerful indeed. Make them work for you, and not against. Let your words be of positivity and attached to the positive side of the force. Speak into the world like citizens of God's kingdom and let yourself experience days of heaven on earth.

It all sounds simple and easy, right? Of course, it's quite the opposite. I personally struggle to always be able to speak only positive words, more so during hard times and high-pressure situations. As well, given my current surroundings (prison), it only serves to add to that struggle. In here, where everything seems hopeless and is at times quite cruel, it's extremely hard to say positive things or to even believe them possible.

The same can be said of situations on the "outside" of the prison walls, where employment issues, financial concerns, relationship struggles, and a plethora of other life issues can bring out the worst in us. In those situations, it's quite easy to fall victim to our feelings of hopelessness and belief in the failures yet to come. Without even a conscious thought, we hear ourselves saying things like, "I'll never find my way out of this," and "I'm not going to succeed," etc.

When we say those things out loud, as the Scripture tells us, we "give birth" to it. We create it unto ourselves and bring it to happen. We engage the negative side of the "faith force" and can only expect those negative words to come true as God said they would.

As people, we are all guilty of saying the things we are thinking. We don't always mean the things we say. Excited utterance, compulsiveness, stupidity, weakness, anger, whatever the cause, the effect is the same. We project it in our own words. Hence, it's so very important to change the way we think and to be repetitive in those ways of thinking so that we come to believe it in our souls and heart.

If we can all learn to speak positive thoughts, then we can, in turn, expect to receive those positive things to come true in time.

But as I said...that begins by changing the way that we think.

Notes:

Raymond E. Lumsden

Chapter 3: **Changing the Way We Think**

How many times have you told yourself, "God can't possibly use me, I'm simply not worthy of anything?" Well, what you may not fully realize is that God never used celebrities, ministers, or those considered "worthy" in the beginning.

Consider that Jacob was a known liar. Moses had a horrible stuttering problem and was without an education. He doubted God and even thought he had a better plan than God. And what about Elijah?

Elijah was suicidal and considered by everyone to be insane. Then there is Timothy, who was only a child and considered by everyone to be far too young to be of value to anyone. Of course, we now know he proved that stigma to be untrue.

We have John the Baptist. This extremely strange man ate bugs and was known to live with the animals. Of course, that made him a good friend for Isaiah, who preached in the nude and would smear his own urine on himself in order to "protect him from the flies."

Rahab was a prostitute and often carried diseases and lice.

And what about the twelve disciples that Jesus chose? All were of very humble means and trade abilities. All are considered unable to bring any change in the world by their fellow man. It makes no sense that Jesus would have selected any of them at all. Many were fisherman, and most were considered social parasites and outcasts in their communities. Even the Roman government, for whom he worked according to Scripture, despised and wanted to kill Matthew. Things were so bad for Matthew as a tax collector that he wasn't even permitted into the synagogue to worship.

Then there is Peter, who was said to have a "foot shaped" mouth.

Just like you and me, all of the men above, chosen by God and Jesus, are full of inadequacies and flaws. Like them, we all have value in spite of those flaws or choices we have made. Therefore, if you should ever doubt your worth to yourself, God, your family, or humanity in general, you can identify with these men, and your faith and self-worth will explode inside you.

Many years ago, computer programmers at IBM coined the phrase "GIGO." No, it's not the insurance company you see on television every day, with "Flo" telling you that you can "save money on car insurance by switching to GEICO."

GIGO, stands for the "garbage in, garbage out" theory. If bad data was put into the program, the results were always bad. If good data was put into the program, then the results were good. Although the acronym is hardly used today, the principle behind it still applies. You can't put in the garbage and expect treasure to come out. Our minds, as we've proven by science and advances in medical understanding, operate just like a computer program, so to speak. We store information, calculate, process, and emit results. If we put garbage into our brains, we will get garbage out of our brains. I'll provide an example.

Perhaps as a child, like me long ago, you were programmed to believe that you were unworthy or "no good" or that you "would never succeed." You may have been told that you were the "devil" or unwanted. You may have been told that you would end up in prison or be a failure. Having heard those things being programmed into your brain, you probably accepted them as fact. And so, based on the "garbage in, garbage out" principle, it's likely it caused you to experience hardships in life. It certainly did in mine.

That being the case, we can delete that old programming and upload a new program into our minds. For example, some very beautiful buildings and houses have been constructed over former garbage dumps and fire damaged areas. Those same areas that were once used for throwing garbage, or burned by fire have been covered with good soil, concrete, or other materials. As time passed and good materials were added, the land became usable again. Our minds can be restored much in the same manner.

You may have used your mind as a dumping ground previously, and you still might be today. But you can rebuild your thoughts and eliminate the old garbage and programming that you once believed in and may still believe.

It is quite easy for our minds to become garbage dumps and full of bad programming. There are many people and sources intending to fill it. It may have been at home, school, juvenile facilities, foster homes, or just on the streets where all of the bad programming and garbage was put into your mind. Some people can be very cruel, and usually due to bad programming of their own somewhere in their past. Even society is guilty of saying things like, "Once a loser, always a loser," or "once a criminal, always a criminal." Some people may have called you a "monster," a "cheater," or whatever it may have been. Some may have wanted to hurt you.

But, according to Scripture, God didn't intend our minds to be garbage dumps or filled with bad programming. We need to carefully test everything we see and hear and eliminate anything that tends to program us with any sense of negativity – television, music, friends, places, etc. We need to protect our minds by continually running a "virus" program that finds and eliminates the bad programs that have been installed into our brains. And the best program for that is, of course, the Bible and Scripture.

The Bible tells us in Philippians 4:6-8:

"Don't worry about anything, but pray and ask God for everything you need, always giving thanks for what you have. And because you belong to Jesus Christ, God's peace will stand guard over all your thoughts and feelings. His peace can do this far better than our human minds."

Our greatest enemy, the devil, is always ready to dump garbage and bad programming into our mind in any way he can. God also wants control of your mind. God is the anti-virus program that can eliminate the bad programming installed by the devil and the people of your past. Of course, from time to time, bad programming and thoughts will pop back into our minds.

One of my all-time favorite motivational authors, Zig Ziglar, used to call this "stinkin thinkin." He said what we need is a "checkup from the neck up." Every day, we will be tempted to dump more bad programming into our minds. This will come from many different places, such as our spouse, friends, family members, television, radio, etc. Our minds are very powerful organisms. What we think, say, and allow into our minds heavily influences who and what we become and how we will live our lives in the future. If we change the programming being input into our minds, we then change the words that will come out of our mouths, thus calling to the positive side of the "faith force."

Amazingly, our minds are always thinking about something, even when we are not consciously guiding it. So, we need to guide our thoughts more carefully whenever we are aware of our thinking. Ask yourself, what thought patterns have gotten you into troubled situations in the past? If you are always drawn to areas of temptation, you should read the Bible Scripture from the letter to Philippians. Train your mind to think about the things Paul listed there. Addictions are known to be forms of compulsive behavior. There are many things we become addicted to, for example:

- Alcohol and drugs
- Tobacco
- Food
- Pain
- Sex

- Gambling
- Pornography

Of course, there are many different kinds and forms of compulsive behavior and addiction. Personally, I found myself addicted to exercise and the use of steroids for most of my adult life. I never used drugs, tobacco, alcohol, and I never gambled, etc. But that doesn't mean that my addiction wasn't real, and that it didn't cause destruction in my life. Without the negative consequences related to the side effects of steroid use, my entire life would be different today.

When we choose to follow Jesus, we tell him that we want him to be in control of our lives. That commitment means that nothing else can control our thoughts or lives. If we are able to identify our compulsive behaviors caused by the bad programming of our past, we can obtain help to overcome them – support groups, counseling, and, more so, prayer. People need God, but we also need other people. So, we must seek help from people, also. God tells us in Galatians 5:19-25:

"The wrong things the sinful self does are clear: committing sexual sin, being morally bad, doing all kinds of shameful things, worshipping false gods, participating in witchcraft, hurting people, causing trouble, being jealous, angry and selfish, causing others to argue and divide, being filled with envy, getting drunk, having wild parties, and sinning in other ways. I warn you now, as I warned you before: The people who do these things will not have a part in God's kingdom. But the fruit a person's spirit produces from birth is love, joy, peace, patience, kindness, goodness, faithfulness, gentleness, and self-control. There is no law against these things. Those who belong to Christ Jesus have crucified their sinful self. They have given up their old selfish feelings and the evil thoughts and things they wanted to do. We get our new life from the spirit, so we should follow the spirit."

The Bible tells us that we must first admit to him through prayer that we are incapable of controlling our compulsive behavior without his help. We must ask Him to help us understand our past in order to better then understand our behavior and thoughts. That all happens in our minds.

God created us with a mind, and he intended for us to use it. Some forms of religion teach that the mind is our enemy. Their followers are told that the mind must be defeated or bypassed in the search for the truth. I have a very hard time understanding that way of thinking, as our minds are an important part of the way God created us. Our mind's ability to learn and function is what brought us out of "the cave," so to speak. It has guided us along the way. I believe God wants to change our minds, not get rid of it. If we weren't supposed to have a mind, we wouldn't have one. In fact, one of the ways Jesus told his followers to show that they loved God was with their minds:

"The man answered, 'Love the Lord your God with all of your heart, all of your soul, all of your strength, and all of your mind.' Also, 'Love your neighbor the same as you love yourself'" Luke 10:27.

Respecting Authority: Boy, if there ever was a problem for me, this is the one. That's mostly because of the bad programming of my childhood associated with authority figures or what I perceived as authority figures. There are too many scars and damage caused by those whom I considered authority figures who programmed me at a young age for the bad. It is something that only maturity, age, and experience have been able to change for me, though I still struggle with this issue more than any other.

Our parents, teachers, police officers, and correctional officers are all considered to be authority figures where applicable. However, since most of those who will be reading this are likely to be incarcerated, I will speak mainly of correctional staff and police officers, though the same ideas and concepts will generally apply to all authority figures.

As a Christian, you are going to relate to many people differently than you ever have before. Your first loyalty will be to Jesus. We are supposed to learn to submit to Jesus once we have accepted him as our savior, which means you now live under his direction. When we submit to his authority, we learn how to live with other authorities in our lives. Where people usually get into trouble, such as me, the underlying problem is usually their attitude towards authority. As humans, we do not like people telling us what to do, which is established inside us from birth. We feel like we should control our own lives, which is instilled inside of us from the "free will" that we obtained through the death of Jesus Christ.

Scripture tells us how we are supposed to relate to authority:

"Be willing to serve the people who have authority in this world. Do this for the Lord. Obey the highest authority. Obey the leaders who are sent by God. They are sent to punish those who do wrong and to praise those who do good. Live like free people, but don't use your freedom as an excuse to do evil. Show respect to all people." 1 Peter 2:13-17

Man-o-man, do I have a problem with that, which has caused me an immense amount of pain and suffering throughout my lifetime? In every aspect of the world, I have been and remain a fighter in heart and spirit. In fact, it is usually my first instinct when wronged or treated unfairly by so-called authority figures, not always in a physically aggressive manner, but almost always in an emotional and mental kind of way. At least, I used to, but maturity and age have had a dramatic effect on me.

That being said, God tells us that we should submit to authority since it was, he who put those structures in place for us. Admittedly, he is right. Not only do we make things harder on ourselves when we go against authority, but according to Scripture, we go against the will of God:

"All of you must obey the government rulers. Everyone who rules were given the power to rule by God's plan. And all those who rule were given that power by God. So, anyone who is against the government is really against something God has commanded. Those who are against the government only bring punishment to themselves. People who do right don't have to fear their rulers. But those who do wrong must fear them. Rulers are God's servants to help you." Romans 13:1-5

Wow! That is going to be a tough one for me, and a lot of you. But I have to admit, it is right, and it makes everything a lot easier.

Our past relationships tend to tell us a lot about our current issues with authority figures, as I mentioned earlier. Especially in my case and quite possibly in yours as well, many of us never had good relationships with one or both of our parents – our first taste of authority. Typically, it was with our fathers. In fact, some of you may not even know your father.

Being fatherless or "parent-less" can scar a young person deeply. This is true even where the parent was "there," but in a bad way. Where it relates to never having had a father, a child is less likely to be able to relate to God as a "Father" in their lives. If your human father did not care for you in the way he should have, you may then question how God could also be a "father" to you. I can tell you without hesitation it is the primary reason that I have struggled with the same concept, as well as with my faith in general. That and the lack of understanding as to how so many bad things could have happened to me as a child. Even as I write this book, sitting in prison for a crime that never happened, I am left with the same questions and doubts. So, certainly, I can then understand any doubt you may have.

But that being said, the Bible speaks of how God cares for us even when our earthly parents do not:

"Even if my mother and father leave me, the Lord will take me in." Psalm 27:10

Even so, children usually form their ideas about how to relate to their authority figures from their parents. Like my own childhood, you may have been beaten or abused. Your parents may have taken advantage of you. In some cases, you may simply have been ignored as if you weren't even there, which can sometimes be even worse. I have always told my own children that silence is the greatest weapon they will ever have in every situation. It makes the mind of the opposition engage with doubt and question, with a lot of apprehension uncertainty, and which in turn leads to self-doubt. As a kid, I hadn't learned this lesson yet and had to learn the hard way when my mouth flew off the handle in defiance, anger, and revenge.

Are you seeing the root of the problem if this happened to you? Can you see how this might influence and impact the way you relate to people in authority today? Parents are supposed to love us. They should provide us with protection, encouragement, and loving correction. If your father, mother, or another adult in authority gave you correction and discipline but did it without love and protection, you likely developed an unhealthy view of authority. I know 100 percent that I did.

I held onto pain and anger, and you might have as well. I rebelled in my own mind because of what I experienced at home and, most of all, in the places I was sent to as a child and teenager. Places meant to "protect" me, nourish me, and provide safety, etc. In reality, they were hell on earth, full of violence, neglect, abuse, and torment, not unlike the way they are to this very day.

Like myself, you may have felt and may still feel like you had to make it on your own in the world. You may have made a vow to yourself that nobody was ever going to hurt you again. So, you learned to hide your emotions, never speak about your pain, or admit how much you are hurting inside. As I indicated previously, you may have turned to drugs, alcohol, or crime since many people do. Perhaps you may have hoped those things would cover your pain and take away your fears and anxiety. And, it may have worked, at least for a little while.

When I was young, I lived with an abusive stepfather. The verbal, mental, and emotional abuse that I sustained along with my brother is beyond what most people can even comprehend. Though the brutal physical beatings left me battered, broken, and bleeding, it was the emotional and mental abuse that did the most damage. The reason for this is simple.

I had developed an apathy – a dulling of the pain from those beatings. At those moments, it wasn't the physical pain that hurt me the most; it was the mental and emotional pain caused by the unreasonableness and insult of the beatings. In that sense, even the blows that didn't land on my body still hurt me. This was a person who was supposed to have loved me, cared for me, protected me, etc. And I'm not just talking about my drunken stepfather. I'm talking about foster parents, juvenile correctional officers, police officers, teachers, etc.

And so, as an adult, around the age of 18, I began training my body in relentless urgency and frequency. My intent was to be so strong, so big and imposing, that nobody would even consider attempting to hurt me. But the damage had already been done mentally, and there was no end to the madness. I simply could not get strong enough or big enough, and so I turned to science to overcome what my DNA had left short. I turned to steroids.

And, from that day, as I had intended, nobody was able to harm me in a physical way again. What I wasn't prepared for was the emotional and psychological pain that normal adult life tends to throw at us. Broken relationships and divorces were mostly caused by my inability to show my love and feelings and harness and eliminate the demons of my childhood. Anger, resentment, fear, lack of understanding, the inability to trust anyone, you name it...I had it. And because of those things, I lost a lot of wonderful people along the way of life. Having said that, however, without the suffering, loss, and growth due to those experiences, I would never have been able to achieve the level of understanding I now pass along in this book.

For me personally, it was the anger stemming from my childhood that remained. I sought a reckoning.

Sometimes, you may become so angry that you feel like a rubber band is ready to snap. But you can learn to control your anger before it explodes and hurts others and yourself. Anger clouds our ability to think positive thoughts in situations and causes us to profess negative words into the world: "Garbage in (anger)...Garbage out (insults, defeat, etc.)." And the more often we become angry and explode with negative outbursts, the more those words go into our ears and into our spirit until we believe them. In believing them, they become true – the laws of attraction.

As a follower of Jesus, we must try to control our anger. Instead of blaming God for the difficulties of life, we should open our hearts and minds to what God is teaching us through those difficult times. God can help you control your tongue and your temper. The worst thing you can do when having a disagreement is to let your anger get out of control. Trust me...I know this better than anyone and wish I had known then what I know now. My past is littered with restraining orders, assaults, inflicted emotional damage, hurt souls and spirits, psychological damage, etc. I was easily triggered and quick to pay for it by losing people that I truly loved very much or cared for, people who had given me their love and trust, and even who had given me my most treasured possessions, my children.

Like myself, you may want to blame someone else for your anger, saying, "They made me angry," or, "It's because they did something to me first." But that is a flat-out lie you are telling yourself. Nobody else can make us lose our temper. The first crime ever committed on earth was murder. It was when Adam and Eve's son, Cain...killed his brother, Abel (Genesis 4:6-7).

And so, we are all capable of becoming angry and hurting both others, and ourselves. We must learn to control it.

Maybe, like myself once again, you carry a lot of guilt and remorse for those that you have hurt in your life. God wants to restore our lives and give us a happy life, but that requires us to first take responsibility for the things we have done. God requires us to be accountable for our past actions and behavior. We must accept responsibility for the pain, hurt, sadness, and grief we have caused others along the way. This is something I had always struggled with up until a few years ago when I began reaching out to some of the people, I have hurt over the years in order to apologize and seek forgiveness, and to pay back the things I had damaged.

I realized through those attempts that apologies simply cannot fix some of those situations, nor will pay back those people. Though I was mostly met with kind reception and acceptance, it wasn't always the case. There are those who will never be able to forget, let alone forgive, and that's okay. That's their right. But whether the person you hurt is willing to accept your apology or not, the change must begin inside of you. You must become aware of the long-term effects of the wrong things you did, as I had to become aware of mine. We must be willing to make things as right as we possibly can, and we must have the courage to make an apology.

We have to accept that we can't undo the past or the damage we caused. We have to try and understand how those people feel as if the things we did to them had been done to us instead. What matters is how you will live your life from here on. The future is the only thing we can change.

Once we accept responsibility for our actions and those we have hurt along the way, we can then find healing inside of ourselves. We can take the next step in righting the wrongs of our life and, at the same time, be doing what God expects us to do...giving and not taking. So, let's talk a little about giving, shall we?

Chapter 4: **Reaping What We Sow**

Scripture says it best in 2 Corinthians 9:6-7:

"He which soweth sparingly shall also reap sparingly, and he which soweth bountifully shall also reap bountifully. Every man according as he purposeth in his heart, so let him give; not grudgingly, or of necessity: for God loveth a cheerful giver."

Imagine what a blessing it would be to our families, friends, and even to strangers and ourselves if we were financially prosperous and more able to help them. Think about what you could do for your community and what a powerful testimony it would be to nonbelievers if you had financial abundance. Suppose you were able to give as much and as often as you wished. It would be awesome, wouldn't it?

Well, it would also be the will of God for us all. According to the Bible, God's will for His people has always been for us to have plenty to enjoy and plenty to give. Even in the Old Testament, He told the Israelites, "There should be no poor amongst you" (Deuteronomy 15:4). The New Testament puts it even more clearly: "God is able to make all grace come to you in abundance so that you may always and under all circumstance and whatever the need be self-sufficient" (2 Corinthians 9:8 Amplified Bible).

Right now, you may be thinking to yourself, "I've asked for such financial blessings, but there must be a catch because I've not received it." As well, you likely know a lot of Christians that are struggling financially, etc. A lot of people have repeatedly asked God for the grace to improve their financial situation, which hasn't happened yet. Or so they believe. In reality, it has happened; they just haven't recognized it.

You were probably expecting a check to arrive in the mail or a promotion at the office. But that's not how God's grace in prosperity works. It now manifests today, just like it initially did in the story of the Macedonian believers in the Apostle Paul's time. Are you familiar with them? If there was ever anyone who needed financial assistance, it was them. They weren't just struggling economically. When Paul went to see them, they were deep in poverty. What did God do to help their situation?

He gave them the opportunity to give in an offering that was being received for the church in Jerusalem. I know, right? What the heck? He put his grace in them by "arousing" them to give, as described in 2 Corinthians 8:1, AMPC).

As Paul wrote: "Though they have been going through much trouble and hard times, their wonderful joy and deep poverty have overflowed in rich generosity. For...they gave not only what they could give but far more. And they did it of their own free will. They begged us again and again for the privilege of sharing in the gifts for the Christians in Jerusalem" (verse 2-4, NLT-96).

Most people today tend to get angry if they hear something like that in today's world. I know I used to until I better understood since I would give freely from my financial abundance. Today, if people find out that a minister or church has allowed some poor believer to give into an offering, they would get very angry and say, "People in that financial situation need to hang onto every penny they have. They don't have enough to give. God certainly doesn't expect them to give."

Actually, the truth is that God does expect them to give, especially if they are believing to prosper. He requires them to give, not because He's trying to get something *from* them but to get something from them. He wants them to activate the spiritual law Jesus talked about in Luke 6:38: "Give, and it shall be given unto you; good measure, pressed down, and shaken together, and running over... "You see...giving activates the receiving cycle according to the Scripture. Of course, you've probably heard the popular scripture, Acts 20:35: "It is more blessed to give than it is to receive." And so, when we give, we're planting financial seeds which will blossom into a financial harvest, essentially breaking us from poverty.

I used to believe that tithing was just a "scam" by the church to get money from people. But over the past couple of years, in my studies of the Bible, and attempt to achieve some semblance of peace in my situation, I began to give. Of course, we don't have real money in prison, but money isn't what the idea is about. There are many types of "financial" giving. And so, when I was preparing a small meal for myself consisting of ramen noodles, tuna, or whatever, I would give it to someone less fortunate and without the financial means to prepare their own meals. I would mail stamps, instead of cash, to churches and places like the Red Cross and Salvation Army.

You see, stamps can be used by various places, such as a dollar, etc. I did this routinely because I was attempting to activate the receiving cycle in Luke because I had been praying for the financial means to hire an appeal attorney to help fight my wrongful conviction and sentence. And I wasn't just asking God for a few dollars, no way, Jose. I was asking him for twenty thousand dollars ($20,000). I know, right? You might as well just be asking for a million. Well...time went on...month after month, year after year...and I was losing faith pretty quickly. And so, one night when I was praying to God before bed, where I normally ask for protection for my kids and for their health, I said to God, "What's the deal? I've followed your words, and I've believed with a repentant and hopeful heart. When are you going to come through for me?"

The very next day, while talking to a friend on the telephone, she tells me, "Ray. So, a while ago, I started seeking donations on your behalf. And I have enough money to hire an appeal attorney. Do you want me to call him, or do you want to have someone else call him?" Imagine the look on my face when she told me that and what I was thinking.

Prior to my arrest, I was a successful business executive earning more than most people can even wish to earn in a year. The entire time, I was of the belief that it was due to my hard work, dedication, and talent at my profession. I was the best earner in the entire country within my field, totaling more than five million dollars in annual sales income for the company. But I realize now that it was more than my skillset that came into play in my success financially. It was my giving.

I have always been a very generous person, giving what I could where I could. Sometimes, at the disapproval of my then spouse. I allowed friends who were going through hard times to live in my home, and I made every Christmas seem like a once-in-a-lifetime event every year. My heart has always been inclined to give and to do for other people financially. Even if I was financially restricted at times, it didn't stop me from giving. I simply enjoy the feeling of making someone feel good with a gift of money, kindness, or assistance.

If you want to hear a more biblical example of how it works, just read Genesis 26 about what happened to Isaac. After Abraham died, Isaac ran into a financial crisis. A famine hit the land of Canaan, and he decided he'd have to move his family to Egypt in order to survive. Before he could implement his plan, God appeared to him to change it. "Don't go to Egypt," he said. "Stay here and dwell in this land." Why did God want him to stay? He said, "I will be with thee, and will bless thee...and I will perform the oath which I swore unto Abraham thy father...and in thy seed shall all the nations of the earth be blessed" (verses 3-4).

That was a far better plan for Isaac. If he stayed, the blessings of God on him could not only prosper him and his family in Canaan, but it could break the famine and bless everyone in the region. It could bring to existence the will of God that" there should be no poor among you." Like I would have done, Isaac went with the plan presented by God. He sowed in that land and received in that same year a hundredfold of harvest. He also began digging out his father's old wells and hit water right in the middle of the terrible drought.

But, because water was so scarce, according to scripture, the Philistines came and took the well away from him. Rather than fight them, he simply gave the well to them and went to dig up another well. Ultimately, because he had chosen to give the well as a blessing, God rewarded him, and Isaac dug into an underground river. Again, I can hear you saying, "Ray, just because God did that for Isaac, you don't mean he will do it for me." Or "Maybe it wasn't God that gave you the money for the lawyer. It was probably just luck or something." My response is that you could be right. But then again...you might also be wrong. That is where faith comes into play and the professing of positive words into the world. I didn't just think these thoughts; I literally spoke to them out loud into the air. My cellmates used to think I was crazy. Not so much anymore...as they, too, have now begun to read the Scripture and profess positive, creative words into the air.

I could be wrong, indeed. But I could also be right. What I know to be one hundred percent right is that I have a great appeal lawyer working on my behalf. So, as for me and my household...we believe. How about another example? A couple of weeks ago, I moved to a different cell in another part of the prison. In doing so, I lost a mini notebook that I use to document personal information, etc. I had looked everywhere for that notebook but was unable to find it. I put the word out that I wanted it returned if found and had the assistance of others in searching for it. From the first night, I began to say out loud, "I will find my notebook." Additionally, I gave a couple of items to an indigent inmate and asked God to return my notebook to me as my reaping.

Last night, I received a few letters from friends, as is usual. But, tied to the top letter with a rubber band was my notebook. I immediately smiled and gave a verbal "thank you" to God because there was no other way it could have happened. Why?

because there aren't particular markings that would give anyone reason to believe that it was my notebook. There simply wasn't any way anyone could have known. Keep in mind that it wasn't returned to me by an inmate who knew I had lost it. Instead, it came from the prison mailroom, without a note or message. Today, when I went to the mailroom to get some legal mail, I asked the mailroom staff about the notebook and thanked them. Both stared at me strangely and said, "What are you talking about, Lumsden? We wouldn't have done it like that. We would have called you to the window and had you identify it."

Mmmm Hmmm...I knew right then and there what had happened. Tonight, I was speaking out loud and praying to God for a big bag of candy for the Halloween season. We shall see what happens (lol). And no, I don't believe in "hocus pocus" type of events or whatever. But I also don't believe we are just floating around in the universe accidentally, helpless, and fully alone, either. I will address this further when I give my personal testimony.

Getting back to my notebook and the blessing bestowed upon me in its being returned to me when reading the Bible, I discovered that God had said in Galatians 3:29 (verses 13-14): "The blessing of Abraham has come upon you."

From my study of Abraham, this "blessing" is extremely powerful. Originally, it started out as the blessing of Adam. It's the creative power and the dominion God bestowed upon us when he said, "Be fruitful, and multiply...and subdue the earth" (Genesis 1:28). When Adam sinned, he destroyed that blessing. But God reinstated it by giving it to Noah and his sons. From there, it became known to Abraham, Isaac, Jacob, Joseph...and eventually to Jesus.

Everything that Jesus did on earth, he did as a prophet under the covenant of Abraham. He never stepped outside of that covenant, and even though he was made in the flesh, he never operated in his divinity. He was made of God and could have...but, he never did. He ministered as the son of man simply operating in the power/blessing of God's word. And just like Abraham and Isaac, that blessing made him rich financially. "Wait, Ray...what are you talking about? Jesus was poor," I can hear you saying. And for a long time I believed the same thing. But, after reading scripture over and over, I've grown to take a different stand. Let me give you my take on it...

First, Jesus wasn't born in a manger because his family was poor. In fact, his father, Joseph, was a businessman of success. He had traveled to Bethlehem so that he could pay his taxes. Did you hear me say "to pay his taxes"? Poor or indigent people do not go around paying taxes. When they arrived, they had to spend the night in a stable, but not for the reason you have been trained to believe. They stayed in the stable for the reason the Bible explains to us in clear language, "[B]ecause all of the hotels were full." There simply were not any other options.

And then came the kings and wealthy men to visit him after his birth. During those visits, after they were told that he was the King of the Jews, those wealthy men gave him "gifts" that were worth a fortune, which Joseph kept: gold, silver, rubies, diamonds, livestock, etc.

When Jesus grew up, he went into the ministry, and his wealth increased. So much so that he required a treasurer to manage his money and property. I'm sorry, but it's my experience that poor and indigent people do not need the services of a treasurer. Also, he owned a sizeable house, gave very extravagant gifts to the poor, and fully supported his ministry team in food, clothing, housing, etc.

Jesus didn't become poor until he was placed on the cross. There, at that point, he took on the curse of poverty. It was on Calvary that Jesus truly and willingly became poor. He did so for you and me so we could be set free from the curse and become joint heirs with him in God's blessings.

"For ye know the grace of our Lord Jesus Christ, that, though he was rich, yet for your sakes he became poor, that ye through his poverty might be rich." 2 Corinthians 8:9

People who know me know that I am a true "textualist," and I stick to the very words written. That, and that I have a very digestive, calculative, and investigative mind. When it came to Jesus, I understood the purpose of it being told that he was "poor" and "indigent." But, in the words of Scripture, it simply isn't true if you look at the text itself. To do otherwise would cast suspicion on the entire Bible and allow the Scriptures to be manipulated and changed to fit the purposes intended. No, the truth of the matter is that Jesus...was born rich...and remained rich up until his being crucified on Calvary. Yes, he was rich in "spirit and eternal life," but he was also rich in financial means as well. Scripture doesn't lie.

Paul was telling us that the degree of financial blessing we walk in is not up to God; it's up to you and me. As a joint heir of the blessings of Abraham, each one of us can sow whatever we want in our hearts, whatever purpose we want to achieve and obtain. We can believe in a hundredfold return and give/sow a lot of seed, or we can give/sow a little and still believe in a hundredfold return on it. As Jesus put it, "[W]ith the same measure that you use, it will be measured back to you" (Luke 6:38, New King James Version).

So, what if you want to give a lot and only have but a little to give? Then you just start where you can and work upwards from there. Simply plant what you can and believe that God, who "ministered seed to the sower," will then "multiply your sown seed, and increase the fruits of your shown righteousness" (2 Corinthians 9:10).

As I stated previously, in relation to my need for funds to hire my appeal attorney and to have my notebook returned to me, how was my giving rewarded in both cases. Of course, those are not the only examples. Think about instances in your own lives where you were up against the wall with bills, worrying how you were going to pay for something, and out of nowhere, everything fell into place. Was it simply by chance? Some sort of "magic?"

Or, if you think about your giving prior to those needs, will it become clear that you have reaped what you had previously sown? Maybe you paid for someone's dinner, mowed your neighbor's lawn, donated property to Goodwill, or put some money into the basket in an offering the previous Sunday at church. In any case, and though you may not even have considered those acts of giving, you had, in fact, sown seeds that required God's blessings. You were then, in His promise, entitled to your reaping/blessing. You see...it works even when you don't realize it.

That is God's plan for all of us if we believe. And since he intends for all of us to be believers, then there shouldn't ever be a poor person among us. It's quite simple,

really, and goes back to the law of attraction, where positive in (giving)...brings positive out (receiving). And the more positive we put in... the more positive we get back.

Managing Your Reapings *(Financial):* Now that you have come to understand the power of giving, there comes with it another requirement, of course: understanding how to manage the reaping you will receive from what you have previously sown. As a follower of Jesus (who also had a treasurer to manage his reapings), we need to recognize a very important fact: following the ways of Jesus is far different than just following the ways of society in general. God owns the world and everything in the world. Even the things we have received from him belong to him, just as we belong to him:

"The earth and everything in it belong to God. The world and all of its people belong to him." Psalm 24: 1

When trying to figure out who we are in relationship to God's world, the word "steward" comes to mind. A steward is someone who helps other people take care of their property. On earth, we are the stewards of God's property. We do not own anything. For example, take our children. We bring them into the world, we love them, we prepare them, we protect them. We call them "ours" when they are young because they are our responsibility. But eventually, the day comes when they pack up and leave us. They become independent and, in time, have children of their own when they themselves become stewards. We don't own them.

The same is true with our property since we will eventually leave it all behind when we die. I've never seen a hearse with a trailer hitch, have you? That's because everything we have in life belongs to God. This was proven to me after a long struggle to believe it when I read the following:

"So, God created humans in his own image. He created them to be like himself. He created them male and female. God blessed them and said to them, Have many children. Fill the earth and take control of it. Rule over the fish in the sea and the birds in the air. Rule over every moving thing on earth." Genesis 1: 27-28

So, being God's stewards, we need to use everything in the world properly, especially the things he has entrusted to us personally. One day, God will require us to show him and account for all of the things he gave us. Money is one of those possessions that God wants us to manage for him.

What does the Bible say about the importance of money? Of the 33 years Jesus spent on this earth, 41 specific days are recorded in the Bible. Here are a few of the facts related to those days that I've been able to find.

On 37 of those days, he talked about money! He talked about money more than he did about heaven and hell...put it together. In 16 of his 38 parables, Jesus talked about money. In the Gospels, one out of every ten verses deal with some aspect of money. The Bible has over four times as many verses on money and material possessions as it has on faith or prayer. So, as you can see, how you manage money seems to be very important to God. Why? Because it's not *your* money...it's *His* money. As I explained in Chapter 2, everything is made up of faith, including money. It's made up of paper or metal, which is made up of molecules, which is made up of atoms, which is made up of subatomic particles, which is made up of faith. And what is faith? It's the substance of things wished for. Money...is the thing people wish for most.

Since God then owns everything, followers of Jesus see money in a different way from the rest of the non-believers:

"Don't ever say to yourself, 'I got all this wealth by my own power and ability.' Remember, the Lord your God is the one who gives you the power to do these things. He does this because he wants to keep the agreement that he made with your ancestors, as he is doing today" (Deuteronomy 8:17-18).

And so, Christians do not view money in the same way everyone else does. There are many forces in the world encouraging us to become voluntary slaves to debts, loans, and material objects. A goal for those who choose to follow Jesus is to become debt-free. God says so in Scripture, of course:

"You shall owe nothing to anyone except that you will always owe love to each other. The person who loves others has done all that the law commands." Romans 13:8

Okay, I hear you...we can't just call up our mortgage company or our bank and say, "I can't make my payment...but...I love you." It would be nice if we could, however. Scripture tells us that where we manage our money properly, we will never be in a position of owing anyone. That we must live within the means that God provides to us.

It's simply a good idea for us to learn how to budget our money so that we can understand how we use that money. The sole purpose of a budget is to help develop a plan to become debt-free. A budget helps us to think like a steward since that is what we are, so that we can give an account for the ways we used God's money on judgment day. Let me ask you this: if Jesus were to walk into your home and ask to see how you manage your finances, what would you say to him? Yep...the old "What would Jesus do" question. But...if you call yourself a Christian and a follower of Jesus, then that's the very question you should always be asking yourself in every situation.

My grandfather used to always tell me that you can learn a lot about a person, including their beliefs and values, by simply looking at their checkbook and appointment calendar. Where do they spend their time and money, etc.? So, let me just ask you...if Jesus looked through your checkbook or your appointment calendar, what do you think he would say? What does he say about the matter? Let's see:

"If you cannot be trusted with worldly riches, you will not be trusted with the true riches of heaven." Luke 16: 11

Ouch! Harsh words, right? Think about that for a while.

Notes:

Chapter 5: Curses – the Sins of our Ancestors

"Like a fleeting sparrow, like a flying sparrow, a curse cannot live without a cause" (Proverbs 26:2).

One of the things I spoke about in the previous chapter that keeps us from the fullness of God's blessings is curses. Curses can only operate against us and our families because there is a legal right for them to be there.

There are five (5) things about curses you should understand:

1) Curses are legal in nature. Consider the Scripture cited above. It has a legal right to operate against you. Proverbs describe a curse as like a bird that is looking for a place to land. God gives us an example of a bird that built its nest on His porch. It was great until the chicks hatched and began to poop on the porch. We let them land, they built a nest or stronghold, and they began to defile everything they came across. The nest was destroyed, but in the next year, the birds returned to build a new one.
The Bible says that curses are like those birds. If you allow them, curses will build a stronghold that will defile everything, and if you are not aggressive, they will keep coming back to destroy and defile everything you have. They return to pollute our lives and our family's lives. Curses are legal in nature; they cannot land and operate without a legal cause to do so.
2) Curses will only be removed in the millennial reign of Jesus. In Galatians 3:13, Jesus, when hung on the cross, became accursed for us, as in "cursed is everyone who hangs on a cross," and that he delivered us from the curse of the law. But Revelation 22:3 tells us that there shall be no more curses. So, when did the curse end? Galatians 3:13 or Revelation 22:3, since both tell us the curse ended?

Galatians 3:13 is the "stated" verdict of the cross. Jesus took away the legal right for curses to operate. He rendered a verdict against curses, if you will, but...if we don't know how to take that verdict and put it into place, curses will continue to operate in our lives. They will deny us the blessings God promised and has in store for us. Frustration will take us since we will continually have bad things happen to us. There will not be a vast "wholesale" release of curses until the time spoken of in Revelation 22:3. Until then, each individual and family has to take what Jesus did and aggressively put it to use. We have to know how to step into the Courts of Heaven and take away the rights that the devil is using to operate these curses against us.

Yes, I realize how ridiculous this sounds, and I struggled against it for most of my life. My grandfather, a Native American, used to speak to me about curses from the time I can even remember. He had owls everywhere in his house to keep away bad "spirits" and curses. As I have become older, I have found these curses to be quite real.

3) Curses are used by the devil to weaken us. Numbers 22:6 tells us the children of Israel are marching through the land, and King Balak sees them and calls Balaam to curse the Israelites because they are too strong for him. And so, Balaam goes to the King. Without curses, we are strong, in fact, too strong for the devil to always defeat us, as in "Stronger that is He who is in us, than he that is in the world," as Scripture tells us. With Jesus, we are stronger, overcomers and survivors.

Sometimes, it may not seem like we are stronger than our enemies because there are curses operating against us, thus stopping the word of God from manifesting inside of us. We need to understand how to undo these curses so that we can step out of fear, weakness, and hardships.

4) Curses are very aggressive. Deuteronomy 28:45 tells us that: "All of these curses will come upon you. They will keep chasing you and catching you until you are destroyed

because you did not listen to what the Lord God told you. You did not obey the commandments and laws that he gave to you. These curses will show people that God judged you and your descendants and forever so. People will be amazed at the terrible things that happen to you." Deuteronomy 28:45-46
Reading Deuteronomy will tell you all about the curses and blessings that God will bring to you. Specific attention to Deuteronomy 28:15-47 will give you a very detailed list of curses that may be imposed upon you, your family, and your descendants. Some of these curses have directly happened to me because of the curses of my ancestors before me. That...is how I know them to be real.

As I said, curses have four (4) states: they come upon you, they pursue you and overtake you, and then they destroy your life. Again, they are very, very aggressive in nature. They will not end until you stop them yourself. You aren't able to "get past" them, trick them, or avoid them. I used to have the attitude that I didn't believe in them and that I was stronger, even if they did exist. But then, one after another, misery after misery, trauma after trauma, drama after drama, hardship after hardship, heartbreak after more heartbreak, something would hit me hard. I had no idea how to stop it because I really didn't believe in it, nor the Bible, to be honest.

Then, one day, as crazy as it sounds, I suddenly "became aware" that there was something working against me – against my family – something very strong and relentless in nature. And so I picked up the Bible and asked God to show me where to look. I literally had no idea where to turn or what to read. So, I just opened the pages and started reading inside of my Bible. It didn't take me long to discover everything written by God about curses. It all came flooding to me, literally, and it all began to make sense.

I began to look back at my childhood and the things that I had endured at such a very young age. Innocent, joyful, smart, and loving in nature, yet so many bad things were forced upon me and happened to me. Having no enemies and not having offended the devil, since I didn't even know who/what the devil even was...there existed only one explanation. I was being struck with the bad curses of my forefathers. They...true to God's word, had found me.

In fact, they had also found my brother, Bill. He also experienced bad things at a young age, having no rational explanation as to why. In fact, the curses had found my entire family...through our bloodline. I just always chalked it up to a bad environment, situations, DNA, etc.

Think about that for a minute or two: curses attack us through situations, environments, bloodline (DNA), and in our lives. The entire time, I was 100 percent right...just not in the sense that I believed it was from a curse or many curses. I get chills to this minute just thinking about it. I had been praying, and my family had been praying for me as well (my grandparents), but nothing worked. Bad stuff kept happening in my life, and nobody, including myself, could understand why.

God said prayer hadn't worked, and here's the reason why. Saul, our predecessor, broke a covenant with the Gideonites. Joshua swore to give them protection, but Saul broke the covenant with them and killed some of them. And because of that, famine had covered the land. So, David went to the Gideonites and said, "What do I have to do in order to fix this?" There, the Gideonites gave him their demands, and David met those demands. At that time, God honored the prayer for the land, and the famine ended because God was now free to answer their prayers because the legal thing that was allowing the famine to operate in the land was removed by David.

Sometimes, prayer alone will not and cannot fix our problems resulting from a curse, but instead, we need to find the legal cause that has brought on the curse and deal with it, and only then will God end it. Yep, I know what you are thinking because I once thought the exact same thing; "How can we possibly know what happened thousands of years ago that caused the curse?" Simple answer: you can't. You see, sometimes it's not just about the actions of our ancestors, but instead, related to our own actions and inactions.

Maybe someone loaned you money in the past. But instead of paying them back when you had the money, you ignored them and went out partying instead. This action would induce the curses promised by God. In order to make it right and defeat the curse, you must make amends with that person and repay the debt. You know...the debt God instructed us not to partake in and create, in Romans 13:8, for example.

(5) Curses can delay and deny our destinies. It is God's intent and desire to bestow his blessings upon us and to upgrade us in spirit. But, sometimes, he is unable to do that because of curses working against us.

When we pray, there are three types of ways to approach God: as our father, as our friend, and as our judge. When we approach him as our father, it is generally based on one of our needs. He is our father; he loves us and cares about our needs. When we approach him as our friend, it is usually in regard to the needs of others. And, when we approach God as our judge, it is usually regarding his purpose in our lives and in the world.

Matthew 6:33 tells us to seek first the Kingdom of God and his righteousness, and all other things will be added to us. Hence, approaching God as our judge should always be our first intention. We need to make his purpose our passion, and everything we need will follow. Why? Because to deny us would require God also to deny himself in order to allow His will to be done, as it is locked up inside of us. If we come to him in His purpose for us, we will see a larger percentage of our prayers being answered. We need to make it about God and His plan. Allow me to give you examples...

In Exodus 32:10-14, Scripture reads:

"Now, therefore, God says, let me alone that my wrath may burn hot against them [the children of Israel], and I may consume them, and I will make you a great nation."

What God is saying is that he is going to consume them, wipe them out, and make a great nation of Moses. God chose Moses for a reason because he was as committed or even more committed to the purpose of God than even God is in this instance. But Moses pleaded with God, "Why does your wrath burn hot against your own people...? "

See what Moses did there? "Your people, whom you have brought out of the land of Egypt with great power and a mighty hand." Moses was reminding God that his purposes are locked inside of each one of us. Moses...presented his "case" to God as our judge. He understood that once we have God's Kingdom in our sights, everything else comes easily to us. The way we present our case to God determines greatly the outcome we can expect. Whether we win or whether we lose. We need to start presenting our needs on the basis of God's plans for us.

I do this every night when I pray to God on behalf of my children and my grandchildren. I always say, "God, if my children and grandchildren become sick, if they fail, or anything happens to them, you are going to lose your purpose in them. Your will shall fail, and your plan for them shall fail. I pray that you protect them and move in their lives so that your purpose can be realized. I pray that you give me the wisdom and knowledge to erase and defeat any curses working through me and against me so that they will not pass onto my bloodline any further."

If your finances are messy, you shouldn't pray, "God, send me some money. I'm broke." No... that wouldn't get you anything. However, what if you said, "Lord, my finances are a mess. I am not a good testimony for you, and I have failed to be your steward on this earth according to your will. I am sorry. I am asking you to move into my finances so that your name will be glorified. So that there is no place in me that could be an embarrassment to you, Amen."

One thing about God is that he likes to have his name and his purpose glorified. He wants us to need him and to want him. He wants us to break free of our selfish, self-centered, "it's all about me" mentality and says, "No God, it is all about you."

When we live our lives according to his plan, he will protect us and show us where our curses exist so that we may defeat them. I personally made a deal with God that if he wipes out any and all curses against me or my bloodline so as to not affect my children and grandchildren, I offer myself as the sacrifice. If my suffering takes the place of my children's, if it will ensure their happiness and success in life...then it's worth every single second of pain, misery, and hardship I have to endure.

Think hard: if your life is in chaos and disarray...who have you offended, and where may your curses exist? Go and make those things right so that God can work his blessings for and through you. If...you aren't sure where the curses might exist, then follow God's will through Jesus...and He will then protect you and defeat them. Pray to Him...move His will.

Prayer against Curses: "Lord, I come before you now seeking your blessings. I want to thank you for everything you have bestowed upon me, both realized...and unrealized. I repent for anywhere I, or anyone in my family or bloodline, may have been in agreement with Baal, intentionally or unintentionally. I repent for my every sexual sin, greed, materialism, failure in your name, and all other shortcomings. I ask for your forgiveness. I ask for the blood of Jesus now to speak for me, my children, my family, and my bloodline before me. When I open my eyes, my path will be of your plan." Amen.

Raymond E. Lumsden

Notes:

Chapter 6: A message to the Incarcerated

Assuming that a large number of the readers of this book will be inmates, and, since I am currently surrounded by inmates, being one myself, I couldn't leave out a chapter specifically designated for you.

You know, even though God created us to be close to him, all of us have messed up that relationship by the many wrong things we have done, none more so than myself in many ways. We are not holy like God. We could not repair our relationship with him, so he sent his Son, Jesus, to bring us back into a good relationship with him. I've noticed that many prisoners do not like themselves very much. Some feel guilty for hurting their families, the people they love, etc. Because of that, combined with the surroundings and conditions of the prison, it is very easy to become lonely, hard, and bitter. It is quite possible that you have decided, "Screw it," saying to yourself, "I don't care what they do to me or what happens to me." Trust me; I see it all around me.

And so, how will that attitude ever lead to you getting out again or finding peace while you are here? Simple answer...it won't. The bad prophecy and words fly out of your mouth, full of negativity and doubt, and then the laws of attraction come into play. Bad in... bad out, remember? The more you profess doubt, lack of hope, and anger, the more your ears hear it...and the more your spirit begins to believe it as true. Your creative power in your words, spewing forth negativity...makes everything you say become reality.

Every single word of this entire book is applicable to inmates, first and foremost. Why? Because we need them the most, and because without them and the knowledge I hoped to teach, we will either never see our freedom again, or we will continue to be a part of the recidivism process.

Every day, I see inmates preaching one thing and doing another. Good men who made mistakes in their lives or failed to correct patterns that would eventually lead them to prison. Kind of like myself, though the reason for my conviction in this situation was false against me. That being said, I am guilty of many other things that could have led me here behind these walls. And so, while I'm here, I want to help as many of you as I can and where I can.

Even if you do not believe that God can love you because of the things you have done, His Word does not change. God still loves you, and he wants the very best for you. If you believe this truth from God's Word, it will make all the difference in your life; I promise you that.

We, as people, cannot stop sinning on our own efforts. We cannot live the way God wants us to by using our own strength. We are separated from God, and that separation will lead to death; I promise you that—either a physical death in this world or a spiritual death in the afterlife.

When Paul wrote to the Romans about death, he was talking about more than our bodies dying; it is much worse than that. It is a death that separates us from God and our loved ones for all eternity. Our bodies may still be alive on earth, but we are without His help or blessings when we do not have faith in Him and do not follow His plan for us.

You might ask, "Can anyone really have a changed life?" And the answer is absolutely. Many inmates have met and come to know Jesus while behind bars and walls. They have allowed him to take control of their lives, and now their entire prison experience and lifestyle have changed for the better. In most cases, that has followed them outside of the prison setting.

Of course, they still face troubles and hardships the same as we all do, but their old ways of handling those situations have changed and are gone. In essence, through believing in Jesus and following His path, they have made a "re-programming" of their minds, as discussed in Chapter 3. Now, they have a positive in... positive out mindset. They are triggering the positive side of the faith force and the positive laws of attraction.

So, where does that knowledge leave you now? At this point, the decision is yours to make. If you want the bad things you have done to be forgiven and a chance at a new life, you must turn away from your old ways and sins. You must make the choice to receive Jesus into your life and have a long talk with God:

- Admit to God that you have sinned against him.
- Thank Him for sending Jesus to die for your sins.
- Ask God to forgive you.
- Tell Him you need him to show you the way and to give you strength.

We are told in 2 Peter 3:9:

"God is being patient with you. He doesn't want anyone to be lost forever. He wants everyone to change their ways and stop sinning."

One of the most important things you can do as an inmate is to find the meaning intended for your life. You see, life isn't primarily a quest for pleasure, nor is it a quest for power, as many inmates have falsely come to believe. Instead, life is supposed to be a quest for meaning. The greatest task for any person, especially an inmate, is to find meaning in his or her life. This can be done in three areas:

- Employment (doing something important)
- Love (caring for another person)
- Courage (overcoming difficult times)

Suffering alone is meaningless; we give our suffering meaning by the way we choose to respond and react to it. A person may remain brave, dignified, and unselfish, or in the bitter fight for self-preservation, he may forget his human dignity and become no better than an animal. Even one instance of a person finding meaning in his life and making the decision to follow Jesus while behind bars is sufficient proof that his inner strength could raise him above and beyond his or her fate.

The outside forces can certainly take away our freedom and liberty, but there is one thing that nothing can ever take away: our freedom to choose how we will respond to the situation. We cannot always control what happens to us in life, especially if we are not walking with God. But we always remain in control of what we feel and do about the things that happen to us.

During my first few months of incarceration, and from what I've noticed about many other inmates here, is the desire and intent to avoid dealing with the truth of the situation. Accepting what has happened to us. For the first few months, I would sleep as much as possible so I didn't have to deal with the situation or my surroundings. I could avoid the misery, pain, and desperation the incarceration brought. In my particular case, I was very angry that I had been convicted of something I hadn't done, let alone even arrested. My anger would overwhelm me to the point that I would literally start shaking.

I understand fully where you may be mentally at this point, regardless of how long you've been in prison. I understand why most inmates either sleep endlessly or turn to drugs and alcohol to stop their minds from thinking.

Recently, I was awakened by the sounds of my cellmate snoring in his sleep. Being unable to sleep myself then, I was just about to wake him up when I realized what I was about to do. Suddenly, I drew back my hand that was in the process of knocking on his bunk. In that instance, I became intensely aware that his dream, even if it were a horrible nightmare, could never be as bad as our situation. And, if his dreams were good, I certainly didn't want to bring him back to his horrible reality.

Trust me, I get it and am right there in the same place. The difference is that I have come to find my purpose in life, which I had previously thought I knew already. In doing so, through faith, I have now found a certain level of peace for whatever may come next, either way.

In my situation, I was not a believer when I entered prison. Quite the opposite, in fact, to be honest. Certainly, I wanted nothing to do with the "circus" that is the prison chapel and religious services program. As I said previously, I simply wanted to sleep and not deal with anyone or anything.

When I slept, my mind still clung to the images of my children and those I loved, wondering where they were, how they were, etc. I realized one sure thing when I slept: love goes very far beyond the physical person of the beloved. It finds its deepest meaning in his spiritual being, his inner self; whether or not he is actually present, whether or not he is still alive at all, ceases to be important.

I did not know what my children were feeling about my absence or how my loved ones were doing at that time, but at that moment, it ceased to matter. There was no need for me to know; nothing could touch the strength of my love, my thoughts, and the image of loved ones, especially my children.

Does that make sense? Can you relate to my feelings? This reflection internally of my life helped me to find refuge from the emptiness, pain, heartbreak, sadness, loneliness, and desolation of my new environment. I was able to escape...through my dreams, into my past life. I could hold my children, see their faces, see my mother and my other family. In my dreams, I drove my truck, went places with my children, walked in the front door of my house, answered my cell phone, turned on my television, ate food from my kitchen, went to work, etc. Those thoughts and visions centered on such details of my life, or the life that I knew, more than once moved me to tears upon waking up and realizing that it was all gone.

But sleeping that much and waking up to immense disappointment and sadness wasn't healthy for me, and I needed to do something about it. So, I picked up my Bible, and I sought out my purpose. I had nothing else left to lose, and everything to gain, and so...I decided to worship.

Worshipping God is a central practice for those following Jesus. When we hear the word "worship" initially, many different ideas come to mind. Some think about going to church or to the prison chapel. Others think about it being related to singing songs. Still, other people think about things in nature, like the stars, etc. Worship can include a lot of these things, but it is much simpler than that while in prison. Here, worship is more of an attitude toward God. If our sins are forgiven, and we have decided to find Jesus and follow Him, we will have lives of worship.

In prison, worship includes confessing your sins to God, obeying God even when you don't feel like it, giving to those less fortunate, praying, or simply giving thanks to God through your actions. Worship can happen any time and place. You can worship standing, sitting, kneeling, or just walking. It can be done silently (my preferred method) or aloud. When we worship, we are simply offering God verbal sacrifice.

"So, through Jesus, we should never stop offering our sacrifice to God. That sacrifice is our praise, and it comes from lips that speak his name." Hebrews 13: 15

When we praise God, we are offering our best gift, even if our minds tend to resist. We are offering our sacrifice. Our minds and lips often don't want to worship, especially in a place like a prison full of distractions. But if you train yourself to worship, you can overcome your sinful ways.

When you are feeling depressed, or you are not feeling well, try worshipping for a brief period of time. As you pray and talk to God, you will notice that it will change how you feel.

Of course, when you try to follow Jesus as a Christian, many problems can get in your way. Some of those problems are experienced by all Christians, but some are unique to prisoners.

Be careful of the following problems, which I learned along my own journey to find Jesus.

1. You expect to grow too fast in your faith and instead don't see the results.
2. You feel that worshipping isn't working because you still feel old habits and sin, so you feel like giving up.
3. You get a lot of peer pressure, and you give up.
4. You feel your prayers aren't being answered, and you're wasting your time.
5. Your life is still a mess, and nothing is going your way, so you feel like giving up.
6. Other so-called "Christians" around you are doing things you don't think are very "Christian," so you feel like giving up.

When you make the decision to follow Jesus in prison, you will also have to take time to work on your attitude toward other inmates. Trust me, this is a hard one. However, conflicts with other inmates can be difficult to avoid.

In the past, how have you handled those conflict situations? Do you become angry and use bad language like everyone else? Do you get into fights? If you answered yes, like I did at the beginning of my incarceration, then it's time to change how you deal with these types of situations.

Keep in mind, which is very hard to do, that Jesus died for your enemies the same as he died for you. God loves those that you consider your enemy.

Often, in prison, arguments become bigger than just using words. How should you react to being threatened or attacked in prison as a Christian? Before I answer, think about how verbal arguments get to this point in the first place. In expressing our anger and due to our ego, we elevate situations that could easily be defused otherwise. Becoming a Christian and following Jesus can reset your entire thinking process and give you the strength to respond in a different way than you normally have/would.

Your old ways of seeking revenge in response to someone hurting you can be reprogrammed with a more positive response. You will be surprised just how much your brain, with the programming of God, can better protect you than your fists.

"But I tell you, love your enemies. Pray for those who treat you badly." Matthew 5~44

That being said, sometimes you might still be physically attacked, even when you do everything right. Don't look for reasons to fight. Many inmates who used to live by violence have learned to live in peace now because they, too, are now followers of Jesus or are trying to be.

As well, prison is depressing enough, and hard enough as it is, without attracting the unwanted reprisals of prison guards. You should never be conspicuous and draw attention to yourself in an unfriendly way. If you do, chances are very high that you will land yourself in far worse conditions.

Many of the fights I've seen in prison actually stem from arguments that either involve politics or religion. Here, you will be exposed to many different views, opinions, and ideas related to Christianity and Jesus. In fact, this book is merely my opinion and thoughts, and you may not even agree with any of it. And that's your right.

Sometimes, other inmates and "Christians" will try to challenge what you believe and what steps you are following in pursuing your faith. Some things are likely to be important to you, but you must learn how God wants you to share them with other inmates. In prison, inmates love to argue, mostly over things they have no real knowledge or experience about. Pride causes arguments because people don't want to admit they are wrong. Or they take great pleasure in proving that someone else is wrong.

Of course, you will encounter a whole lot of inmates who claim to be following Christ but have false beliefs and are involved in everything bad that takes place. These are the inmates that you want to pray for but completely avoid.

Reading the Bible can also help you overcome and deal with the excessive noise of prison life. It will bring you inner peace. If you do not feel peaceful in your mind, the sounds around you may bother you even more. It's not uncommon to find me in my cell, reading the Bible or studying legal books and materials. Reading can drown out the noise as you focus on the words, especially when reading the Bible, where you have to pay closer attention to the writings in order to obtain their meaning.

Most importantly even if you find that religion just isn't for you, that doesn't mean that the principles about religion won't be helpful to you. I said it previously, and I will say it again...anything positive that you can upload into your mind only results in positive things coming out of your mind.

And in prison, the more positiveness you have...the better off you will be. The truth is, I seldom ever speak to other inmates about religion, if ever. I assist with legal work, letters, educational assignments, advice, etc. I share life experiences, I try to keep hope alive inside of others as best I can, and I try to make it a better place for everyone.

There is no reason why you cannot do the same. In fact, perhaps you should.

Raymond E. Lumsden

Notes:

Chapter 7: **Author Testimony**

And so, here we are. If I were to receive a nickel for every time I have been asked about my religious beliefs over the course of my life, I'd be a multi-billionaire. That has been truer during my terms of incarceration, where other inmates are seeking out some form of hope, reassurance, guidance, and love...but just aren't sure as to the validity of the subject.

Being then aware of that pursuit and understanding that I stick out from the "normal" prisoner due to my educational background, elevated intelligence, life accomplishments and experiences, and overall demeanor and disposition, I have intentionally avoided the subject altogether.

Most prisoners come from a life of drug abuse, alcohol abuse, limited educational background, challenged intelligence, low acumen, and poor economic status. The hardships, struggles, and social environments in their lives, for whatever reason, led many prisoners to turn to habit-forming substances at an early age. Also, most dropped out of school in their teens. I've come across many prisoners who struggle with verified mental illness and disabilities as well. In all cases, the reason I have specifically and intentionally avoided the subject of religion is to not give a false idea or perception. Plus...I was simply "on the fence" about the subject.

I know that many prisoners are very impressionable, and I didn't want to be responsible for their spiritual failures, lest that be the case. Also, I didn't want to be perceived in the eyes of God as a hypocrite if I were wrong. As I said, my attitude and opinion about religion changed hour-to-hour, day-to-day, etc. Which, of course, is why I have never discussed the topic with my own children. Then, of course, they have never asked me, and that, I suspect, is because religion is something we often hear about first from our parents.

And so, I guess it may be best to simply start from the very beginning. The first recollection that I have regarding religion was from my step-grandmother, Florence. My mother had married my stepfather when I was only two years old, so I had always known my step-grandmother as simply my real biological grandmother. Florence, was her first name, and I will simply now refer to her as "Grandma Florence."

Grandma Florence attended the local Church of Christ in the small town of Worthington, Minnesota, where I mostly grew up during my childhood. Not only did she attend the church, but she also worked there. As a kid between the ages of 2 and 10, I would sometimes go and "help" her do things around the church, such as vacuuming, cleaning windows and mop floors, cleaning the pews, etc. I truly did enjoy going and helping out, mostly because afterward, I was always treated to a McDonald's meal, which was a true rarity for me as a kid due to our financial status at home.

Not only did I savor the Big Mac combo meal, but I also got to have a caramel sundae afterward. Of course, that wasn't all I enjoyed since that time with Grandma Florence was mostly filled with her stories, questions, and laughter. She was such a fun, kind, warm, and affectionate woman to us, even though there was a biological difference between us.

During that time, Grandma Florence would talk about Jesus and faith. As a young kid, I remember the stories she told, combined with the stories I'd heard at "Church School," which we attended every Sunday as kids, to be a lot like the stories of Santa Claus, Easter Bunny, etc. They seemed very grandiose in nature and a little unimaginable, though it interested me, nonetheless.

I can still remember sitting in the church, looking at the enormous-sized statue of Jesus hanging on the cross, which was affixed to the wall behind the pulpit, and feeling... "something." Perhaps induced by the stories of Grandma Florence mixed with Sunday School and being so young, I always felt like there was "someone" in that Church with us, even when it was just us. I would sit staring at the face of Jesus and could have sworn that he was not only looking at me but...speaking to me telepathically. It made me feel so uncomfortable, yet at the same time, I also felt a sense of peace.

On Sundays, the church would always sing songs like "The Old Rugged Cross," "Amazing Grace," and "I Exalt Thee." Of course, Grandma Florence was the loudest singer in the entire church, which sometimes embarrassed me. But, during those songs, I can remember feeling as if I would somehow be struck by lightning if I didn't sing along. It was a ridiculous notion even for a kid, but nonetheless, I sang.

While I sang, my eyes were always "pulled" to that statue of Jesus hanging high on that wall, as if he were judging me and unhappy with me for some reason. And I had viable information to believe that he was, considering he could see everything, hear everything, and would punish me for bad acts, a lot like Santa Claus. The best way for me to describe it would be to compare it to the feeling one would get when your dad would look at you when he was certain that you had done wrong, not in anger, but in disappointment.

On the other side of town lived my Grandma Isabelle, whom I lovingly called "Grandma Issy" as a kid. Hands down, Grandma Issy was my favorite person next to my mother when I was growing up, followed very closely by my Grandpa Ray (Issy's husband) and Grandma Florence. Grandpa Ray was my true biological grandfather, but Grandma Issy was not biologically related to me. That being said, it didn't matter to me whatsoever because, in my eyes, I didn't know any different.

Grandma Issy, a lot like my Grandma Florence, was a devout Christian and attended church every Sunday and Wednesday. Her home had photos of Jesus on nearly every wall, and on the dashboard of her car sat a moving statue of Jesus and the Virgin Mary. Whenever I saw Grandma Issy or went to their home, she always had a loving smile, gave us a warm hug, and was always singing. To this day, I have never known a person to pray as much as my Grandma Issy did. Mostly, it was for me and my siblings.

Grandpa Ray and Grandma Issy were the parents of my biological father, a father I had very little contact with growing up. Grandpa Ray was not very fond of him for many reasons, mostly for the way that he had abandoned my mother, my brother, and me. At any rate, as a kid, I did not have a very good opinion about my biological father, mostly because I never knew him.

Either way, my introduction to Jesus and religion came at an early age due to the influences of my grandmothers., However, my introduction to Satan and Hell also came at an early age, courtesy of my drunken stepfather.

As a kid, when hearing our pastor speak or read the Bible myself, I was always perplexed about the way that God claimed to love us. At the same time, he punished us with plague, disease, famine, atrocities, and death. It reminded me a lot of the home environment I was then growing up in with my stepfather, which was very confusing to my young mind. On the one hand, he taught us a lot of things, would take us hunting and fishing, throw the football around with us, etc. On the other hand, he would administer severe verbal, mental, and emotional victimization while he also delivered beatings so horrific that I was left bleeding, bruised, and with broken bones.

Though it was more than 30 years ago now, I can still remember some of the thoughts I would have had during those beatings as my mind went to a place in search of understanding. Most of the beatings we were subjected to took place in my childhood home on Strait Avenue, which had numerous photos of Jesus placed throughout, having been gifted to my mother from Grandma Issy. I wonder today if those photos were given to her in an attempt to, in some way, calm everything in the home. If that was the intention, it certainly didn't work.

One of those photographs was of Jesus looking toward the sky, hands folded in prayer, with the light from heaven shining down on him. During one specific beating, I remember looking at that photo and thinking that Jesus was praying for me, praying that the beatings would stop. And, in my mind, as every punch landed on me, I was also asking God to help me.

But…he never did, and the beatings never stopped. In fact, they became more frequent and severe. God had abandoned me in my worst moments, or so I was left to believe. But the beatings from my stepfather weren't the only reason I needed God at that time.

Somewhere around the age of 8 years old, I began being sexually abused by an older female neighbor. I remember she sent me to the local store once to get her some milk and a pack of Salem cigarettes. Back in those days, children could buy cigarettes without any problems. I can remember the brand name because they reminded me of a television show my mother would watch sometimes called "Salem's Lot."

After delivering the items, I was sitting on the couch watching cartoons. The woman sat beside me, and within a few minutes, the abuse began. It would continue for years until we moved to a different home across town. When we moved into the new home, it wasn't long before the abuse began again by one of my elementary teachers who lived "nearby."

What I remember about those instances, in both situations, were things in my surroundings, when my mind would go elsewhere in an attempt to thwart the things being done to me and the things I was being forced to do to them. I can specifically remember both women having photographs of Jesus in their homes. One had a photo of Jesus holding a rod, leading sheep in a pasture, and walking towards one sheep that was separated and surrounded by wolves. I can remember feeling as though I was that separated sheep during those times. That photo was hanging on the wall next to the window in her bedroom where I could see my house, where my mother was at the time.

Having been taught to "keep my mouth shut" about the beatings from my stepfather, since my mother was unaware of most of them and thought my injuries were mostly from playing rough with friends and fighting, I never told a soul about what those women were doing and had done to me.

I also came to hate Jesus and God, for that matter, which had both left me to the wolves, so to speak. It was my young opinion that this type of God, who would allow this kind of thing to happen to a kid, was no God of mine. And that the entire "story" around religion was just that...a story.

As time went on, as well as the beatings and molestations, I began to act out in school, as well as everywhere else. For me, learning came easy, and I had little trouble with homework and school assignments. More often than not, I would finish the work so quickly that I was left with the worst thing I could have...time to think. When that would happen, in an attempt to push away the thoughts, pain, embarrassment, anger, etc., I would act out in bad ways.

Damage to property, fighting, theft, curfew violations, you name it...I did it. I literally had no other recourse in letting out what was inside of me. That, and sports which I excelled at more so than anything else, and understandably so. Football, basketball, track, martial arts...I could outperform anyone my age, as well as much older. The beatings of my stepfather had made me physically strong, as well as highly aggressive and durable. I had been fine-tuned into the perfect athlete, and "competition" was something I craved and needed.

But, my attitude and behavior would always prevent me from maximizing my full potential or from participating in events due to being suspended from my school or being sent to juvenile facilities or foster homes. This only served to fuel my religious disenfranchisement and contempt towards God, if I believed in God at all.

In the summer of 1986, I was sent to my first juvenile detention center, located in the furthest northern part of the state of Minnesota in the thick of the forest, called Thistledew Youth Camp. This was the first time I had been away from my hometown, friends, school, etc. And the first time I had ever been away from my most favorite person in the world...my mother.

It could easily be said that I blamed God for everything because, in truth, I actually did. I hated him for not protecting me, for allowing everything to happen as it were, for even allowing me to have been born at all.

Recently, I obtained a copy of the "commitment order" that was provided to Thistledew Youth Camp by the sentencing judge, along with a letter that said the following:

"Raymond has come to the attention of this court for many delinquent behaviors on several occasions in the past couple of years. His parents have consistently refused any counseling offered by this court and the Nobles County Family Services Agency, thus leaving me no choice but to impose the current punishment. Raymond is a very intelligent, bright, and likable boy who has, in my belief, been through horrible living conditions rampant with extreme physical, mental, and emotional abuse. I am, at this point, unable to help him further and am left with no other alternative than to now commit him to Thistledew in hopes of having some sort of positive effect on him. Unfortunately, upon his release from Thistledew and return to his home, I fear that situation will only serve to further diminish the light of this pleasant young man's future."

In other words, as I interpret it, the judge knew of my stepfather's abuse and was furthering my punishment in spite of it. Indeed, as the Bible instructs, it was a case of "The sins of the fathers," indeed as well as the sins of the judge for doing the worst thing he could have done for me.

Let me tell you about juvenile facilities in the 1980s:

On the way to Thistledew Youth Camp, I was shackled to another kid we had picked up in a neighboring town, who was a couple of years older than me. I first noticed the trees and the long driveway leading up to the facility's front door. Thistledew was on a large and sprawling estate and totally encompassed by pine trees, birch trees, and a lake. It was out in the middle of nowhere, about twenty miles from the nearest town, which made escaping possible...but futile. Trust me, I thought about it.

Add to that the fact that there were wolves, bears, and other things like bobcats, moose, and mountain lions all around...and so I was trapped. My stomach moved with fear of the unknown, homesickness, and anger as we pulled up in front of the intake building.

Upon getting out of the police car, the other kid and I were turned over to a man in his 60s, whom we were told to call "Sweed." He wasn't very imposing in size and seemed to be kind. But appearances are deceiving. I immediately noticed the black lab dog that was accompanying Sweed without it being on a chain. The dog's name was "Max."

Max came over to me, tail wagging, and naturally, I reached down to pet him. At that moment, Sweed struck me on the arm with the walking stick he had in his hand and said, "Never, ever touch Max unless I tell you to." I was both in shock and scared to death. Not because the blow had hurt me, since my stepfather had done far worse, but because of the insult of expecting a boy to not instinctively want to pet a dog.

After Sheriff Peters had left us, we were brought into Sweed's office in an older cabin-like building. There, we were stripped completely naked, made to stand directly in front of him, and told to recite the Lord's Prayer. When we stood there confused, without doing as instructed, Sweed let out a booming voice, "Say the Lord's Prayer, Damn It!"

Instinctively, I began saying the prayer out loud. The other boy, who I later knew to be named Kyle, unfortunately, did not know the Lord's Prayer by heart. Because of that, he received a few very stiff blows to his naked body from Sweed's stick. That incident was the first time something related to God, or religion, ever proved important and saved me, but not for long.

"Turn around, bend over, spread your cheeks," Sweed instructed us. It was the first time I had ever been instructed to do anything like that in front of a grown man or in view of another kid. I was horrified, to say the least. In tears, shaken, scared to death, humiliated, I did as I was told, fearing a repeat of what had happened to Kyle with Sweed's stick. When the contraband inspection was done, Sweed moved to the next step in the process, the "compliance" lesson. We were told, "turn around, place your hands on the floor, with your ass in the air." After complying, the "lesson" began.

Sweed systematically, moving between Kyle and myself, delivered hard blows of his belt to our naked butts. Of course, it wasn't the first time I had been spanked with a belt, not even on a naked butt, but it was the first time a stranger had done so. The entire time he hit us, we were made to say, "I will do as I am told," over and over again until the blows stopped.

At the end of the initiation process by Sweed, Kyle, and I were taken into the dormitory area where all of the other boys were, and we were assigned to our specific group and bunk. I was assigned to the "Stumpjumper" group in bunk #27. I remember thinking to myself, 27...is the same day that I was born (November 27); it must be fate. Being nighttime, we were all told to "prepare for lights out," which meant putting on our pajamas, getting into bed, and not talking. Just before I began to get into my state-provided pajamas, I heard a voice behind me say, "Not you...I have other plans for you."

I was taken out in the dark, behind the dormitory, where the other boys were preparing to sleep. I was handed a long saw, a steel maul, and a can of red spray paint. There were trees everywhere, and I was told, "Go and get a tree...cut it into 14" sections, split it, spray it red, and stack it in this crate until it reaches the top. (This is known as a "rick" of wood).

It took me more than three hours to cut that rick of wood, which was the method of punishment best used by the guards for disciplinary action, and where it normally only took the other boys about forty-five minutes to cut. The reason for my extended length of time in cutting it was that I was made to cut it completely naked while the mosquitos savaged my body, which had been sprayed with sugar water by the officer in charge that night. After I had completed the cutting, I was allowed to shower and was told by the officer that I had been made to do that because "He saw the devil in me, and defiance."

During the next four months, the beatings and cruelty that we all had been subjected to by those who were supposed to provide "direction and protection" inflicted a whole new level of hate inside of me, pushing me even further from God.

I would eventually be released from Thistledew Youth Camp and return to my home in Worthington, Minnesota. Now, in place of the young kid that had left previously stood a well-muscularized thirteen-year-old from all of the wood chopping and cutting, full of hate, distrust, and contempt. This only served to infuriate my stepfather further. And so, within hours of my being home, he and I were face-to-face, toe-to-toe, in the center of our living room, preparing to battle. In the end, the defiance was beaten out of me, having been a little challenged by the strength and ferocity of my very strong and capable stepfather. Everything had returned to "normal" at home.

Just a few months later, after I had been beaten so badly that both of my eyes were swollen shut and my tooth knocked completely out of my mouth, I hatched a plan to steal a car and run away. What ended up happening was I did steal the car but never left town. Instead, a few friends and I took that stolen car and drove out to the home of the judge who had sent me away (or at least we thought it was his home) and tore up the front yard. I was caught and subsequently sentenced to a "harsher" juvenile facility.

In 1988, I was sent to the Sauk Centre Juvenile Correctional Center. I had made it the worst of the worst. I had heard the stories while at Thistledew and had pledged never to be sent there. Yet here I stood at the front door. After the Sheriff left, I was taken to a building known as "Sullivan," which was known to be the disciplinary building. There, I was once again given a "welcome" ceremony by the attending guard, which consisted of being taken into a solitary confinement cell, having duct tape put across my mouth, and then being beaten with a "strap" while I was handcuffed to the bed.

I remained in that solitary confinement cell for about a week until I was considered "compliant" and released to another cottage called "Stowe." In Stowe cottage, housed with far more advanced "city" kids from St. Paul, Minneapolis, etc., I grew up faster than I was prepared to or mentally able to do. The first night, while lying in bed, I heard the other boys laughing. When I opened my eyes to see what was going on, I realized that I had been tied to my bed with pieces of sheets. Two older boys stood over me, masturbating until they ejaculated on my blanket. Then, with soap inside of their socks, they began to beat me all over the body, avoiding the face. This was considered a sign of initiation, and you only received the respect of the other boys if you didn't cry out or snitch on them afterward. I never cried, and I never snitched.

During that stint at Sauk Centre, I was subjected to far more cruelty than I had ever been subjected to by anyone, hands down, second to none. Some of which I have never spoken about to anyone and will not do so in this book. What I will tell you is that once, I had prayed to God and offered the following,

"Lord, I am going to run away. If you let me see my Mom again, I promise to do what you want me to do. If not, just kill me right now." A few nights later, when returning home from a movie outing in town for good behavior, our van lost control in a bad winter storm. A few of my friends and staff died in that accident. My friend, Brian Kester of St. Peter, Minnesota, who had also been at Thistledew with me, was decapitated in the crash.

I woke up in the hospital with a broken collarbone and bruising. Once I was allowed to leave, I was returned to the facility, where the atrocities done to us quickly picked up again. I was released a couple of weeks later but would return in just a few months when I was turning 16. Of course, this time, I had no intention of staying. And so, accompanied by a friend, Levi, I snuck out of the cottage and climbed the chicken wire fence that then surrounded the facility with the assistance of two forks taped together and a doormat to throw across the razor wire at the top of the fence, and escaped.

After having broken into someone's home in an attempt to obtain warm clothes since it was winter and a vehicle to drive back home in, I was eventually caught and returned to Sauk Centre. While being held in Sullivan Cottage isolation, I tied a sheet around my neck and attempted to kill myself, again, for the third time in my life up to that point. I nearly got the job done but was discovered by the security "rover" before it was too late. I was taken to the local hospital, treated, and released. Because of that escape, I was taken to St. Cloud, Minnesota, and charged with burglary and car theft.

While I was there in juvenile holding, I met my assigned lawyer. During that discussion, he said, "I can get you home tomorrow; all you have to do is sign here to be an adult." And so, wanting to get back to my newborn son, Anthony, I signed the paper...thus entering my life as an adult in the eyes of the system.

During those years as a kid, and into my teens, and though I "hated" God, I continued to pray to him. I continued to seek him out in moments of very hard times and hurl insults at him when things didn't go right. As well...I read the Bible when I was locked up, just as I read Danielle Steele novels and educational books. Why? because I wanted it to be true. I wanted to believe that it was true, in spite of my instincts that it wasn't. I wanted to belong to a "family" like the ones described in both the Danielle Steele books and the Bible. I wanted a father who was there and who would bleed *for* me instead of making *me* bleed.

As a young adult, I had the desire to have a family of my own and to seek out the love that I had never known but always wanted to propel me into hundreds of sexual and dating relationships prior to my marriage and also during those marriages. The problem was, I didn't know how to properly love a woman, nor had I the tools to do so. All I knew were my demons, which I was then, and always, trying to outrun – the nightmares, the anger, the fear, the sadness, the distrust of everyone and everything.

I was physically fit, good-looking, charming, intelligent, and savvy, and I had a great sense of humor and a generous heart. I had very little trouble attracting women to me. In fact, I had no trouble at all, which only made it all worse. Nothing about my relationships with women happened slowly. They did not "burn" slowly or evenly like a good fire should. Instead, they would ignite quickly and explosively at first start and then end in the same way, with an explosion. It's exactly like throwing gasoline onto a fire...Poof! There was no turning back.

Sex was secondhand to me for many reasons. I had a child with a 19-year-old woman when I was just fifteen, nearly sixteen. And she was far from my first sexual partner. The women of my childhood had "taught" me things of a sexual nature that most men never learn how to do, let alone men in my age range at the time. The ecstasy, emotional, and physical happiness that I could bring to a female partner was limitless and only added to my personal charm and character. Because of that, the women of my past fell hard and fast, as I did in some instances. But...the demons weren't done with me yet.

In every single relationship I've ever had, I subjected those women to a blend of psychological, emotional, mental, and spiritual assault, and, in a couple of instances, even physical. All of this stemmed from, and was a direct result of, my childhood upbringing and abuses.

All of those women, to this day, are beautiful, wonderful, amazing, and talented. The problem was that I was full of the "wrong stuff" emotionally, psychologically, and spiritually. I cheated on them, insulted them at times, ignored them at times, rejected them at times, and would then do the exact opposite. I would love them, whisper sweet things, buy them gifts, hold hands, spend time with them, inspire and encourage them, tell them they were beautiful, etc. It was a rollercoaster from hell for both of us in all the serious cases. Of course, there were those that were simply for "fun," in which we got along fine and are still close to this day.

All that being said, it also went both ways in many cases. I was on the receiving end of some physical abuse, cheating, psychological episodes, and insults administered by a few of these women. Some because I apparently "made them crazy," and others because they were just as crazy and damaged in certain ways as I was. It was the perfect storm, so to speak.

Where God was concerned, with every failed relationship and every one of my hardships, I blamed and rebuked him. The more I hated him, the more hardships seemed to rain down on me. I just couldn't understand any of it.

In fact, a few of my former female partners, including my last wife, had a strong faith and attended church regularly. Of course, I ridiculed her sweet, beautiful, wonderful self for even mentioning the word "God" in my presence. When she did, I would do everything to convince her that it was all a myth and complete crap. I could see that it literally destroyed her when I did that, and I carry a lot of guilt and remorse because of it. The truth is, I have never met a happier, funny, more peaceful, and mature woman. I am glad our marriage ended because she deserved much better than what I could ever give to her at that time. That being said, losing her scarred me very deeply, and I will never forgive myself, even if she finds it in her heart to do so. If you ever read this, Brandy, I am very sorry.

My greatest source of failure, sadness, regret, and shame comes from my relationship with my wife of nearly fifteen years (all included). In essence, we basically grew up together since we met when she was 18 and I was 25. I won't go into great detail out of respect for her, but we sure went through it all together. The hell that I put that woman through, the cheating, the late nights out, the times I ignored her, the various forms of abuse she suffered because of me, and in spite of me, make her eligible for the title of Sainthood. If you ever read this, Amanda, I am very sorry.

Where past relationships are concerned, none erupted as quickly and intensely as did my relationship with my youngest daughter's mother. Wow, did it happen with the full ferocity one can only hope for. But, due to the woes of both of our pasts and childhood experiences, most of which fall on me, it ended just as quickly and passionately. Lyndsey was just 25 years old at the time we met, and at age 40, I had no real business with her despite everything else. She had our daughter, Rylee, a year after we met, and her life was changed forever. Lyndsey, if you ever read this, I am very sorry.

Often, I am judged based on my past relationships and actions. I have, in the deepest sense of the word, harbored great regret for so many things in my life. But in my defense, I submit that no man should judge me unless he first asks himself whether, in a similar upbringing or in similar situations, he may have made the same choices and done the same things. I certainly do not believe that I am the mere exception to the laws of attraction or to circumstances beyond our control. It is very difficult for those who did not grow up as I did...or experience the same hardships as I did...to understand how very little value and self-worth I harbored. During my time in juvenile facilities and jails, I was considered a number and not a person. I was addressed by that number and never by my name. I had no worth as a person. I counted only because I had that assigned number, much like right now. Dead or alive, it is unimportant. All that mattered in relation to me was that I was counted on the ledger – that my number matched the count sheet.

Throughout my account of juvenile life, in attempting to understand the psychological and emotional characteristics suffered, I may present that my life was just influenced by my surroundings and conditions. But what about human liberty? Is there no spiritual freedom in regard to behavior and reaction to any given surrounding? Is the theory true, which would have us believe that Man is no more than a product of our conditional and environmental factors, whether biological, psychological, or sociological in nature? Are we simply the accidental product of these things? These are questions I have always been in search of answers to because I truly wanted my life to be different, and I tried hard to make it so without success.

I have always lived my life under the popular quote by Nietzsche: "Was mich nicht umbringst, macht mich starker." (That which does not kill me makes me stronger.) And so, as my life has gone on, failure after failure, hardship after hardship, I was simply becoming stronger. That strength was responsible for many wonderful things in my life.

For instance, I had a lot of great relationships with women, which, in truth, exceeded all of the bad ones tenfold. I have loved, been loved, I have been blessed with life friends, and most of all...I was blessed with four amazing children (Anthony, Alyssa, Joshua, Rylee). I have known a lot of love along the way and in spite of my demons.

74

Love was once explained to me by a woman as "Grasping another person in the innermost core of their personality." Nobody can become fully aware of the essence of another person unless they first love themselves. By the love we have for ourselves, we are then able to see the traits and features in those that we love and even more, we can see the potential in them. Sex is merely a mode of expression of love, but not love itself, which took me most of my life to figure out. Sex is justified as soon as possible, but only as long as it is a vehicle of that love. Sex should never be used as a means to find love in the absence of that love (Alyssa and Rylee, you better listen to your Dad here).

My entire life, the reason I failed in my relationships was because I believed that sex...would bring love and that it was love. And so, when love never came after the sex, I grew upset, frustrated, and blamed the woman. It has taken me forty years to understand why people have always said to save sex until after marriage. People like...God.

Had I waited to have sex with all of those women, it is very likely that I could have avoided a lot of heartache and pain for all of us. Also, I could very likely have found a very strong and long-term love that could have lasted a lifetime. That being said, let me make it perfectly clear that in no way do I regret having sex in some of those situations since that is how I was able to bring my wonderful children into the world, even in the absence of true love with their mother, where applicable. In the instances of my children, the absence of love, or any suffering I may have experienced in spite of that absence, ceased to be suffering the moment it found meaning, such as the meaning of sacrifice and being their father.

Now, I'm not saying that suffering is necessary to find meaning since I did, at the time, love their mothers as much as I was capable of loving them. I'm only saying that meaning is possible even in spite of any suffering, provided that the suffering is unavoidable. Let me give an example...

My daughter, Rylee, was born around 28 weeks prematurely. The chances of her survival were not very good at the time. During the next 12 weeks, she was in the Neonatal Intensive Care Unit (NICU), and my heart was suffering far more than it ever had previously. As I looked down at her, I prayed with all of my heart that she would make it, making deals with God, offering myself in her place, etc. The suffering, at that point, was unavoidable; therefore, it was necessary to find meaning. That meaning...was made clear to me at that very moment. My purpose in life was made clear to me at that point as well, though it took me a while and another hardship to achieve it.

My children, hands down, are my greatest source of pride, love, and accomplishment. Nothing that they could ever do or have ever done could impede or change that. In the case of Rylee, I will share with you something that I have never told a soul before this, not even Rylee or her mother.

When it wasn't highly expected that Rylee would live...I went down to the hospital chapel, closed the door, and turned out the lights. I hit my knees, closed my eyes, and spoke to God. Since Rylee was a child, if she were to die, she would have been worthy of the highest place in Heaven, according to Scripture. But, for myself, as a sinner, I could not expect to be sent to the same place in Heaven, therefore, never being able to see her again. And so, I said to God, "Please don't take my child from me. I have suffered in my life enough to pay for her life now. I offer that as payment for her life."

At that time, I had made the decision already that if Rylee died, the only recourse for me to ever see her again in Heaven was through my own suffering since I had read that in a Bible one night when I was sitting next to Rylee in the NICU. Psalms 56:8 had me believe that I could suffer enough to purify myself, therefore making me worthy of joining her in Heaven.

"But what about your other kids, Ray?" (I hear you say that). My other kids were alive and would be able to make their own destinies in their lives. Having been born, they were already sinners in the eyes of God but could redeem themselves later. Rylee would never have gotten that chance. I realize the craziness it entails and the strangeness of the story. But...I truly felt that way at the time, I was prepared to suffer.

Think about that, as is the case with all of the hardships I had endured throughout my life when I was distant from God and rebuked the very mention of his name. When the crap hit the fan, he was the first person I reached for. Why? Because I always knew he was there in spite of myself. That's why I was mad at him in the first place. I mean, who gets mad at someone who isn't there? You can't hate anything or nobody, right?

As I stand today, I am verifiably convinced that we have the potential within ourselves, and the potential we actualize depends on the decisions we make in spite of various conditions, not because of them. My childhood certainly didn't prepare me for being a responsible adult, and I failed a lot. On the same note, I have experienced a lot of financial success, friendships, love, travels, journeys, and children despite that childhood and the atrocities related to it. I know now that we have the gift to choose. We get to choose our faith, our partners, our lives, and everything else we want. Nothing simply happens in spite of our choices. Nothing!

Happiness cannot be pursued; it must be ensured. We require a reason to be happy. Once that reason is found, happiness happens without further action. It's like laughter; if you want to make someone laugh, you must provide a reason for them to laugh, right? Once you do that, they will laugh without having to take any further action. You cannot force or will someone to laugh. If you do, it's like saying "cheese" before taking a photograph. It looks strained and fake on their faces. The same applies to happiness. If you are truly happy, a smile and laughter are automatic. In the absence of true happiness, there is only a fake smile and a fake laugh.

As people, once we find meaning in our lives, it leaves us happy and also gives us the ability to cope and overcome hardship and suffering. On the flip side, and in addition to that, I can honestly say without hesitation without the suffering and hardships, including this time in prison, the growth and understanding that I have achieved, including my faith, would have been impossible. Raymond Lumsden is no more than the sum of all the hurt, pain, diversity, struggle, and hardships I have had to face and endure. I am strong because of it and in spite of it.

For most of my life, perhaps I suffered from Dunning-Krueger Syndrome. It is a syndrome that makes us ignorant of facts, making us think we know more and are smarter about situations than we truly are. It's a repetitive cycle in that the same ignorance that causes a person's failures and poor performance is also responsible for how we view ourselves in those situations. We believe that we are better than we actually are and that we are merely victims.

While I may, in fact, have been a victim as a child, and perhaps even a little in my adulthood, I made very bad choices. Though some of my behavior was reactionary and explainable, it was also irresponsible and unacceptable. I was exercising the negative side of the faith force, and in response, I received negative experiences and consequences, like my current situation.

In the present, I sit in prison for a crime that never happened and which resulted from another failed relationship with a woman, however innocent and slight it may have been. I made choices, and because of those choices, I projected negative faith into the world, which required negative punishment. Garbage in... garbage out. God is punishing me.

Of course, nobody should ever be imprisoned for false allegations or for wrongful and unjust means. It leaves things infirm and cannot stand under the rules of God. And so, I put my faith in Him to make things right and to bring me justice. If He has punished me for past indiscretions, then I now accept that punishment until He decides I have paid enough for them. I will continue to grow in my faith to overcome the human qualities that lead to my inadequacies and failures.

I am a sinner and have always been a sinner. But, as long as my heart continues to beat, I have the opportunity to redeem myself so that I become worthy to enter Heaven one day, not because of the streets of gold or the fear of burning for eternity. Instead, I seek the Kingdom of Heaven because that is where my precious children will be one day after I am gone, along with my mother and everyone I have loved and still love most. I want to be with them for eternity. I want to meet my children at Heaven's Gate to see their faces when they arrive.

I choose to believe. I choose to become the person and father my children would expect me to be. The father that my youngest child Rylee always thought me to be and that my oldest daughter Alyssa used to believe I was.

If I'm wrong...then I have lost nothing. But, if I am right (and I am), I have gained everything.

I ask you now to walk with me...I'd like to see you all in Heaven one day as well. If you believe, you can achieve.

God Bless.

Raymond E. Lumsden

Notes:

80

About the Author

Raymond Lumsden is currently an inmate in the state of Texas, where he is aggressively fighting his wrongful conviction and unjust sentence.

Currently participating in numerous faith-based correspondence programs, he strives every day to realize the changes he wishes to see in himself and the world.

A father of four wonderful children and with three grandchildren, he understands his obligation and duty to make the world a better place for them.

He begins this by spreading hope, light, and change to those around him who need it most…inmates.

Mr. Lumsden is the author of numerous books currently available, with more coming soon.

Raymond E. Lumsden

Ask. Believe. Receive

FREEBIRD PUBLISHERS

Pro Se Collection by Raymond E. Lumsden

This legal collection is the no-nonsense, easy to understand, and effective work by one of Freebird Publisher's Best Selling Legal Authors, Raymond E. Lumsden. Specifically written by an inmate with extensive legal training and education, for inmates seeking relief in the twisting and confusing legal system of America.

★ Easy to follow instructions;
★ Dozens of sample motions and pleadings;
★ Up to date case citings and writings;
★ **5** Star Amazon Ratings;
★ Numerous success stories of relief being obtained, etc.

A MUST HAVE COLLECTION FOR ANY PRO SE USER!!!

We accept all forms of payment!

★ COMING SOON ★
- *The Pro Se Guide to Parole*
- *"DNA": Proving Your Innocence*

PayPal
VISA DISCOVER BANK
venmo Cash App
@FreebirdPublishers $FreebirdPublishers

For more info on each book, order our catalog!

CATALOG ONLY $5 - SHIPS BY FIRST CLASS MAIL
We have created four different versions of our new catalog A: Complete B:No Pen Pal Content C:No Sexy Photo Content D:No Pen Pal and Sexy Content. Available in full Color or B&W (please specify) please make sure you order the correct catalog based on your prison mail room regulations. We are not responsible for rejected or lost in the mail catalogs. Send SASE for payment by stamp options.
ADDITIONAL OPTION: add $5 for Shipping with Tracking

NO ORDER FORM NEEDED CLEARLY WRITE ON PAPER & SEND PAYMENT TO:
FREEBIRD PUBLSIHERS 221 Pearl St., Ste. 541, North Dighton, MA 02764
www.Freebird Publishers.com Diane@FreebirdPublishers.com Text/Phone: 774-406-8682

CURRENT FULL COLOR CATALOG

92-Pages filled with books, gifts and services for prisoners

We have created four different versions of our new catalog A: Complete B:No Pen Pal Content C:No Sexy Photo Content D:No Pen Pal and Sexy Content. Available in full Color or B&W (please specify) please make sure you order the correct catalog based on your prison mail room regulations. We are not responsible for rejected or lost in the mail catalogs. Send SASE for info on stamp options.

Freebird Publishers Book Selection Includes:

- Ask. Believe. Receive.: Our Power to Create Our Own Destiny
- Celebrity Female Star Power
- Cell Chef 1 & 2
- Cellpreneur: The Millionaire Prisoner's Guidebook
- Chapter 7 Bankruptcy: Seven Steps to Financial Freedom
- Convicted Creations Cookbook
- Cooking With Hot Water
- DIY for Prisoners
- Federal Rules of Criminal Procedures Pocket Guide
- Federal Rules of Evidence Pocket Guide
- Fine Dining Cookbook 1, 2, 3
- Freebird Publisher's Gift Look Book
- Get Money: Self Educate, Get Rich, & Enjoy Life (3 book series)
- Habeas Corpus Manual
- Hobo Pete and the Ghost Train
- Hot Girl Safari: Non-Nude Photo Book
- How to Write a Good Letter From Prison
- Ineffective Assistance of Counsel
- Inmate Shopper
- Inmate Shopper Censored
- Introduction to Financial Success
- Kitty Kat: Adult Entertainment Resource Book
- Life With a Record
- Locked Down Cookin'
- Locked Up Love Letters: Becoming the Perfect Pen Pal
- Parent to Parent: Raising Children from Prison
- Penacon Presents: The Prisoners Guide to Being a Perfect Pen Pal
- Pen Pal Success: The Ultimate Guide to Getting & Keeping Pen Pals
- Pen Pals: A Personal Guide for Prisoners
- Pillow Talk: Adult Non-Nude Photo Book
- Post-Conviction Relief Series (Books 1-7)
- Prison Health Handbook
- Prison Legal Guide
- Prison Picasso
- Prisoner's Communication Guidelines for Navigating in Prison
- Prisonyland Adult Coloring Book
- Pro Se Guide to Legal Research & Writing
- Pro Se Prisoner: How to Buy Stocks and Bitcoin
- Pro Se Section 1983 Manual
- Section 2254 Pro Se Guide to Winning Federal Relief
- Soft Shots: Adult Non-Nude Photo Book
- The Best 500 Non-Profit Organizations for Prisoners & Their Families
- Weight Loss Unlocked
- Write & Get Paid

PayPal

CATALOG ONLY $5 - SHIPS BY FIRST CLASS MAIL
ADDITIONAL OPTION: add $5 for Shipping and Handling with Tracking

NO ORDER FORM NEEDED CLEARLY WRITE ON PAPER & SEND PAYMENT TO:
FREEBIRD PUBLISHERS 221 Pearl St., Ste. 541, North Dighton, MA 02764
www.FreebirdPublishers.com Diane@FreebirdPublishers.com Text/Phone: 774-406-8682
We accept all forms of payment. Plus Venmo & CashApp! Venmo: @FreebirdPublishers · CashApp: $FreebirdPublishers

FREEBIRD PUBLISHERS

Thanks for your interest in Freebird Publishers!

We value our customers and would love to hear from you! Reviews are an important part in bringing you quality publications. We love hearing from our readers-rather it's good or bad (though we strive for the best)!

If you could take the time to review/rate any publication you've purchased with Freebird Publishers we would appreciate it!

If your loved one uses Amazon, have them post your review on the books you've read. This will help us tremendously, in providing future publications that are even more useful to our readers and growing our business.

Amazon works off of a 5 star rating system. When having your loved one rate us be sure to give them your chosen star number as well as a written review. Though written reviews aren't required, we truly appreciate hearing from you.

Sample Review Received on Inmate Shopper

poeticsunshine

★★★★★ **Truly a guide**

Reviewed in the United States on June 29, 2023

Verified Purchase

This book is a powerhouse of information. My son had to calm/ground himself to prioritize where to start.

www.ingramcontent.com/pod-product-compliance
Lightning Source LLC
Chambersburg PA
CBHW071104090426
42737CB00013B/2470